U.S. Geological Survey
Rewarding Environment Culture Study, 2002

By Janis C. Nash, Carol A. Paradise-Tornow, Vicki K. Gray, Sarah P. Griffin-Bemis, Pamela R. Agnew, and Nicole M. Bouchet

Open-File Report 2006–1192

U.S. Department of the Interior
U.S. Geological Survey

U.S. Department of the Interior
KEN SALAZAR, Secretary

U.S. Geological Survey
Marcia K. McNutt, Director

U.S. Geological Survey, Reston, Virginia: 2010

For more information on the USGS—the Federal source for science about the Earth, its natural and living resources, natural hazards, and the environment, visit http://www.usgs.gov or call 1-888-ASK-USGS

For an overview of USGS information products, including maps, imagery, and publications, visit http://www.usgs.gov/pubprod

Suggested citation:
Nash, J.C., Paradise-Tornow, C.A., Gray, V.K., Griffin-Bemis, S.P., Agnew, P.R., and Bouchet, N.M., 2010, U.S. Geological Survey Rewarding Environment Culture Study, 2002: U.S. Geological Survey Open-File Report 2006–1192, 50 p., available only online.

Preface

This U.S. Geological Survey (USGS) Open-File Report 2006–1192 contains references to internal USGS documents and Web sites to which public access is not available. Copies may be made available upon request.

A rewarding USGS environment is one in which employees are motivated and energized to produce outstanding science and science support and are valued and recognized for their contributions.

—From a USGS Rewards Summit of managers and employees in October 2000

Contents

Figures

Tables

U.S. Geological Survey Rewarding Environment Culture Study, 2002

By Janis C. Nash,[1] Carol A. Paradise-Tornow,[2] Vicki K. Gray,[3] Sarah P. Griffin-Bemis,[4] Pamela R. Agnew,[4] and Nicole M. Bouchet[1]

Executive Summary

"The underpinning of the scientific credibility and respect of the USGS [U.S. Geological Survey] has been its talented staff."

National Research Council, 2001, p. 126

In its 2001 review of the U.S. Geological Survey (USGS), the National Research Council (NRC, p. 126) cautioned that "high-quality personnel are essential for developing high-quality science information" and urged the USGS to "devote substantial efforts to recruiting and retaining excellent staff."

Recognizing the importance of the NRC recommendation, the USGS has committed time and resources to create a rewarding work environment with the goal of achieving the following *valued outcomes*:

- USGS science vitality

- Customer satisfaction with USGS products and services

- Employee perceptions of the USGS as a rewarding place to work

- Heightened employee morale and commitment

- The ability to recruit and retain employees with critical skills

To determine whether this investment of time and resources was proving to be successful, the USGS Human Resources Office conducted a Rewarding Environment Culture Study to answer the following four questions.

- **Question 1:** Does a rewarding work environment lead to the *valued outcomes* (identified above) that the USGS is seeking?

- **Question 2:** Which management, supervisory, and leadership behaviors contribute most to creating a rewarding work environment and to achieving the *valued outcomes* that the USGS is seeking?

- **Question 3:** Do USGS employees perceive that the USGS is a rewarding place to work?

- **Question 4:** What actions can and should be taken to enhance the USGS work environment?

To begin the study, a conceptual model of a rewarding USGS environment was developed to test assumptions about a rewarding work environment. The Rewarding Environment model identifies the *key components* that are thought to contribute to a rewarding work environment and the *valued outcomes* that are thought to result from having a rewarding work environment. The 2002 Organizational Assessment Survey (OAS) was used as the primary data source for the study because it provided the most readily available data. Additional survey data were included as they became available.

---

[1]U.S. Geological Survey, former employee.

[2]Consultant, Tucson, Ariz.

[3]U.S. Geological Survey, San Diego, Calif.

[4]U.S. Geological Survey, Reston, Va.

Question 1: Does a Rewarding Work Environment Lead to the *Valued Outcomes* That the USGS is Seeking?

To determine whether a rewarding work environment leads to the *valued outcomes* that the USGS is seeking, questions from the 2002 OAS were linked to each of the *key components* and *valued outcomes*. Multiple regression analyses of employee responses to those questions were run to test the Rewarding Environment model.

Findings.—Results of these analyses supported the Rewarding Environment model and indicated that the *key components* of a rewarding work environment contribute to employee perceptions of the USGS as a rewarding place to work and lead to the *valued outcomes* that the USGS is seeking.

The analyses also identified the top 10 *key components* of a rewarding work environment that have the greatest impact on the *valued outcomes*. In rank order, these *key components* are:

1. Rewards practices
2. Fairness and respect
3. Risk-taking
4. The work itself
5. Overall supervision
6. Performance management
7. Communications
8. Skills and training
9. Resources
10. Managing diversity

Significance.—All of these *key components*, except "the work itself," are directly related to the working environment established by managers and supervisors. Because these *key components* are under the direct control of managers and supervisors, they represent areas of opportunity for enhancing the USGS work environment.

Question 2: Which Management, Supervisory, and Leadership Behaviors Contribute Most to Creating a Rewarding Work Environment and to Achieving the *Valued Outcomes* That the USGS is Seeking?

To identify the behaviors that contribute most to a rewarding work environment, USGS science centers and offices were ranked on the basis of their employees' average response to the 2002 OAS statement: "Overall, I find USGS a rewarding place to work." The 15 science centers and offices that ranked highest on this statement and the 15 that ranked lowest were identified. These data were then used to profile the differences between the science centers ranked as high versus those ranked as low on this outcome.

Findings.—The highest and lowest ranked science centers and offices were found to differ significantly on nearly all of the *key components* and *valued outcomes* of a rewarding work environment.

Managers and supervisors in science centers and offices that ranked highest as a rewarding place to work were found to be more likely than other managers and supervisors to do the following:

- Create an environment that fosters and supports science excellence

- Focus on goals and objectives of the USGS and hold themselves and their employees accountable for achieving positive results

- Demonstrate fairness and respect, support risk-taking, and encourage others

- Collaborate and communicate effectively

- Provide the training needed by employees and recognize employees for their contributions

Science centers and offices that ranked highest as a rewarding place to work also were more likely than other science centers and offices to achieve the following *valued outcomes*:

- High ratings on the health and long-term viability of their science

- High levels of employee pride and commitment

- The ability to recruit and retain employees with critical skills

Significance.—The behaviors identified in the study that contribute to a rewarding work environment can be used by managers and supervisors as a practical guide to the types of actions that can be taken to enhance the work environment in their science centers and offices.

Question 3: Do USGS Employees Perceive That the USGS is a Rewarding Place to Work?

To assess whether the USGS is a rewarding place to work, the Rewarding Environment model and the 2002 OAS results were used to create a Rewarding Environment status report. The report indicated that the USGS has achieved progress both in creating a rewarding work environment and in achieving the *valued outcomes* that the USGS is seeking. Each *key component* and *valued outcome* was linked to one or more OAS questions, and employee favorable responses to the corresponding OAS question(s) were averaged. A score was then determined for each *key component* and *valued outcome*, with the score expressed as a percentage of favorable (F) responses.

Findings.—The Rewarding Environment status report identified the *key components* and *valued outcomes* most favorably and least favorably rated by employees as of the date of the 2002 OAS.

Most favorably rated:

- Employee perceptions of customer satisfaction (80 percent F)

- Quality-of-worklife flexibility (78 percent F)

- The work itself (73 percent F)

- Resources (65 percent F)

- Managing diversity (64 percent F)

- Security and safety (63 percent F)

- USGS as a rewarding place to work (63 percent F)

Least favorably rated:

- Fairness and respect (45 percent F)

- Communication (43 percent F)

- Risk-taking (43 percent F)

- USGS science vitality as rated by research scientists (43 percent F)

- Rewards practices (41 percent F)

- Employee morale and commitment (41 percent F)

- USGS science vision (33 percent F)

- Operational support (33 percent F)

- USGS ability to recruit and retain needed talent (29 percent F)

Significance.—The 2002 OAS findings indicate that while a majority of employees found the USGS to be a rewarding place to work at the time of the survey, employee perceptions were related more to the satisfaction they found in the work itself rather than the work environment established by their managers and supervisors.

Question 4: What Actions Can and Should be Taken To Enhance the USGS Work Environment?

A four-quadrant Rewarding Environment priority matrix was developed as a tool to determine top priority actions for enhancing the USGS work environment. The Rewarding Environment status report **score** for each *key component* and the **impact** of that *key component* on a rewarding work environment were plotted to determine the relative priority for action. Low-scoring, high-impact *key components* plotted in the quadrant labeled "top priority." These represent the *key components* that are in the greatest need of improvement and, if improved, would have the greatest relative impact on the overall levels of employee satisfaction with the USGS work environment.

Findings.—The Rewarding Environment priority matrix identified eight *key components* of a rewarding work environment as top priority for action by the USGS. In rank order, these eight *key components* are:

1. Rewards practices
2. Fairness and respect
3. Risk-taking
4. Overall supervision
5. Performance management
6. Communications
7. Skills and training
8. USGS science vision

Significance.—Results of the 2002 OAS indicated that while employees recognize that their managers and supervisors play a pivotal role in creating a rewarding work environment, employees believe that their managers and supervisors could be doing more to enhance the current work environment. By identifying the *key components* of the work environment that have the greatest need for improvement and the greatest return on investment, the Rewarding Environment priority matrix provides USGS senior leaders, managers, and supervisors a blueprint for taking action.

Recommendations

As with any culture change, creating a rewarding work environment is an ongoing process that takes leadership and continuing focus in order to institutionalize the change. Senior leaders, managers, and supervisors play critical roles in reinforcing a rewarding environment culture in the USGS.

Senior leaders are responsible for setting the example of a rewarding work environment for managers, supervisors, and employees. Senior leaders should take the following actions:

- Model the behaviors that create a rewarding work environment

- Develop the leadership and management skills of managers and supervisors

- Communicate expectations of senior management and hold managers and supervisors accountable for creating a rewarding work environment

- Recognize managers and supervisors for their accomplishments

Managers and supervisors have the primary, day-to-day responsibility for creating a rewarding work environment in their science centers and offices. Using the Rewarding Environment priority matrix as a guide, managers and supervisors should take the following actions:

- Engage employees in a dialogue about what makes the work environment rewarding for them and take action to address the issues identified

- Recognize and reward employees based on merit

- Demonstrate fairness and respect in dealing with all employees

- Discuss performance expectations and provide performance feedback

- Trust employees to take responsible risks

- Use available resources to learn about creating a rewarding environment and put that learning into practice

- Encourage employees to participate in the next OAS and discuss the results with employees

The dividends of creating a rewarding work environment can be great. As the results of the USGS Rewarding Environment Culture Study of 2002 indicate, creating a rewarding work environment is an investment that can have an important impact on the outcomes that the USGS values—the vitality of our science, the satisfaction of our customers, and the morale, commitment, and performance of our employees.

I. Introduction

In its 2001 review of the U.S. Geological Survey (USGS), the National Research Council (NRC, p. 126) observed that "the underpinning of the scientific credibility and respect of the USGS has been its talented staff." The NRC (2001, p. 126) cautioned that "high-quality personnel are essential for developing high-quality science information" and urged the USGS to "devote substantial efforts to recruiting and retaining excellent staff."

Recognizing the importance of the NRC recommendation, the USGS has focused attention on and invested resources in creating a rewarding work environment in order to achieve the following *valued outcomes*:

- USGS science vitality

- Customer satisfaction with USGS products and services

- Employee perceptions of the USGS as a rewarding place to work

- Heightened employee morale and commitment

- The ability to recruit and retain employees with critical skills

In 2002, the USGS Human Resources Office initiated a Rewarding Environment Culture Study to assess the return on the investment made by the USGS in creating a rewarding work environment. The return on the USGS investment of resources was evaluated by answering the following questions:

- **Question 1:** Does a rewarding work environment lead to the *valued outcomes* (identified above) that the USGS is seeking?

- **Question 2:** Which management, supervisory, and leadership behaviors contribute most to creating a rewarding work environment and to achieving the *valued outcomes* that the USGS is seeking?

- **Question 3:** Do USGS employees perceive that the USGS is a rewarding place to work? Why or why not? Do these opinions vary across regions, disciplines, or other groupings?

- **Question 4:** What actions can and should be taken to enhance the USGS work environment?

The purpose of this report is to describe the "baseline" state of the USGS rewarding work environment, using 2002 Organizational Assessment Survey (OAS) data and 2002 hard data[5] of Rewarding Environment actions and outcomes. This report also identifies *key components* that define and contribute to a Rewarding Environment culture and examines the relations between those components and the *valued outcomes* identified above. Based on study findings, recommendations are presented regarding actions that USGS managers and supervisors can take to enhance the Rewarding Environment culture in their science centers and offices and the actions that should be taken by the USGS in the next phase of the Rewarding Environment culture change effort.

The findings, success stories, implementation challenges, and recommendations in this report reflect the status of the USGS and the Rewarding Environment culture in 2002.

Background

The USGS Strategic Plan (U.S. Geological Survey, 1999) identified rewards as a critical challenge facing the USGS and set a goal of revamping the rewards system to increase equity and better align rewards with the USGS strategic direction. Employees affirmed this assessment by ranking rewards as one of the areas of greatest concern on the 1999 OAS.

In response to the Strategic Plan and the 1999 OAS results, the USGS convened a Rewards Summit of managers and employees in October 2000 to examine rewards issues and to revamp the USGS rewards system. After reviewing USGS rewards practices and OAS results, summit participants agreed that the USGS already had in place ample traditional reward mechanisms. Rather, the group determined that the rewards issues facing the USGS stemmed from an over-reliance on cash awards and promotions, a decrease in motivational value of cash awards based on how and when cash awards are given, and a lack of perceived linkage between rewards and merit. Recognizing that external research indicates that employee motivation, morale, and performance can best be achieved by using a full spectrum of rewards in the work environment (Manas and Graham, 2002),

---

[5]These data include a variety of existing business and (or) science performance data that already are being collected.

summit participants created the concept of a *Rewarding Environment*, which encompasses everything in the work environment that employees value and find rewarding.

Rewarding Environment as a Culture Change Effort

Summit participants recognized that creating a rewarding work environment was not a new program or process but rather a culture change—a change from a culture focused on monetary awards to one that uses the full array of workplace rewards to create an environment in which employees are motivated to deliver outstanding science and science support. Figure 1 provides an overview of the change model (Linkage Inc., 2009) that was used to guide the Rewarding Environment culture change effort.

Consistent with the change model (fig. 1), the following actions have been taken to guide the Rewarding Environment culture change:

- **Making the case for change.** The USGS Strategic Plan and 1999 OAS results identified the need for change, and the 2002 OAS results confirmed this assessment. The Rewarding Environment research presented in this report strengthens the case for change by demonstrating the connection between a Rewarding Environment culture and the vitality of USGS science.

- **Enlisting stakeholders to develop a vision.** Summit participants developed the Rewarding Environment vision, strategy, and actions necessary to carry out the culture change. A Rewarding Environment Program Manager was appointed and a Rewarding Environment Team was established to provide direction and to design an approach to move the Rewarding Environment culture change out into the organization. The Deputy Director served as Bureau champion for Rewarding Environment, and a manager champion was designated in each region and at headquarters to assist the Regional Directors and Deputy Director in implementing the culture change.

- **Communicating the vision.** The USGS Executive Leadership Team (ELT) launched the Rewarding Environment culture change by communicating the Rewarding Environment vision. Using training developed by the Rewarding Environment Team, three ELT members trained their ELT colleagues on Rewarding Environment concepts. Following this training, ELT members communicated the Rewarding Environment message to their direct reports, who, in turn, were then responsible for communicating the message to their subordinate supervisors, and so on throughout all levels of the organization. A Rewarding Environment Handbook and Web site were created, and Rewarding Environment concepts were incorporated into USGS supervisory and leadership training and the mentoring and orientation programs to ensure that the Rewarding Environment vision and message were communicated to a wide audience across the Bureau.

- **Removing barriers.** Challenges and barriers to the Rewarding Environment culture change, described in detail in section IV of this report, were identified by managers, supervisors, and employees during Rewarding Environment training. These challenges have been addressed in the supervisory and leadership training programs in which Rewarding Environment concepts have been incorporated. Recommendations for additional steps that can be taken to minimize or remove barriers are presented in section VI of this report.

- **Setting milestones and acknowledging progress.** To kick off bureauwide implementation of the Rewarding Environment culture change, the Deputy Director, manager champions, Rewarding Environment Team, and regional Human Resources specialists held a Rewarding Environment Workshop to establish milestones and to develop an implementation plan for each region and headquarters. A Rewarding Environment Measurement Plan was developed to assess the effectiveness of the Rewarding Environment culture change effort, and Rewarding Environment success stories were collected and published on the internal USGS Rewarding Environment Web site to acknowledge progress. (See section IV for additional information regarding success stories.)

- **Reinforcing the change.** Research findings concerning the impact of a Rewarding Environment culture on science vitality have been incorporated into supervisory and leadership training to reinforce the importance of the culture change.

The Rewarding Environment culture change effort depends on individual managers and supervisors to create a rewarding work environment for the USGS. This study identifies the management, supervisory, and leadership behaviors that are most critical to achieving a Rewarding Environment culture and the *valued outcomes* that a Rewarding Environment culture helps to support and promote.

The Linkage© 6-Phase Change Process[1]   USGS RE Culture Change Effort

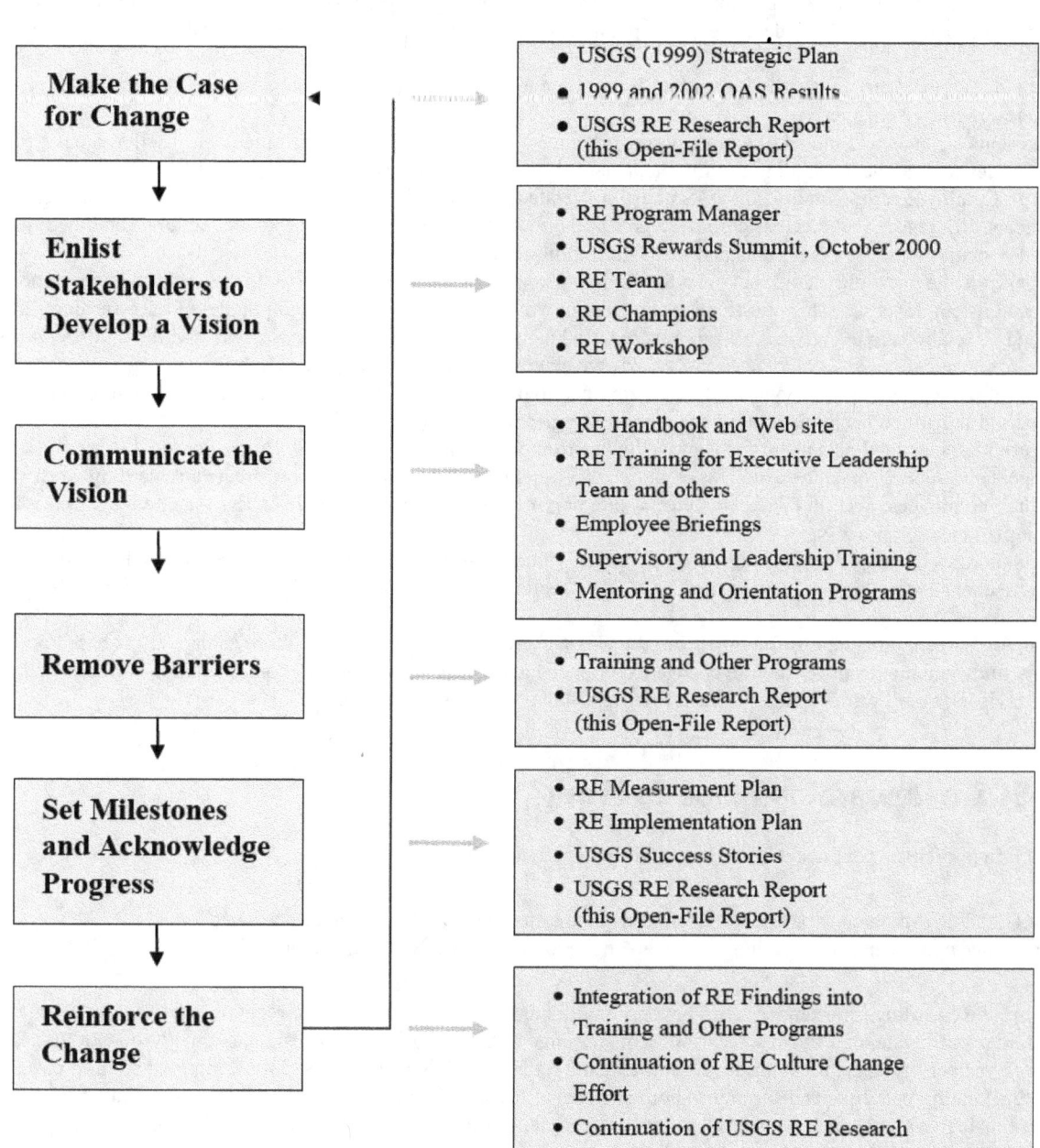

[1]Copyrighted by Linkage, Inc., 2009, "Change Leadership: Tools and Techniques for Leading Downstream and Upstream Change," Burlington, Mass. Used with permission.

Figure 1.   Overview of the change model used to guide the Rewarding Environment (RE) culture change effort in the U.S. Geological Survey (USGS). OAS, Organizational Assessment Survey.

Overview of This Report

This report contains six sections plus appendixes. Sections I through VI provide the research results, study conclusions, and recommendations. Appendixes A through F describe and explain the research process, including the methodology used for this study.

Section I provides the background for the Rewarding Environment culture change effort and describes the actions taken at each of the six stages of culture change.

Section II presents a conceptual model of a rewarding work environment at the USGS. The model was used as a basis for this research and for developing the Rewarding Environment status report, which answers the question: "Is the USGS a rewarding place to work?" Employee responses to 2002 OAS questions related to Rewarding Environment are summarized and examined, as are significant differences found across employee groups. Hard data on Rewarding Environment actions and outcomes are reported, and the relations between these data and the OAS findings are discussed.

Section III answers the question: "Does having a Rewarding Environment make a difference in outcomes that are important to the USGS and its employees?" This question is answered in two ways. First, the conceptual model of a Rewarding Environment culture and its relations to the *valued outcomes* were tested using the 2002 OAS results. Second, significant differences in Rewarding Environment culture and outcomes between science centers and offices ranked as "High Rewarding Environment" and those ranked as "Low Rewarding Environment" were examined to determine if overall Rewarding Environment ratings provided any meaningful distinctions in outcomes between the two groups.

Section IV provides anecdotal data about the Rewarding Environment culture change in the form of success stories reported by managers and supervisors across the USGS who have implemented innovative ways to create a rewarding work environment for their employees. Section IV also includes a summary of the key challenges and barriers that have been encountered during the implementation process.

Section V summarizes the major conclusions derived from this study and their implications for carrying the Rewarding Environment culture change effort forward within the USGS. This section also serves as a foundation for the recommendations that follow.

Section VI presents recommendations for enhancing the USGS Rewarding Environment culture change effort based on the findings of this study and the results of culture change experienced at other organizations. Recommendations are directed to managers and supervisors, the Rewarding Environment Program Manager, and senior leaders.

II. Is the USGS a Rewarding Place To Work?

Rewards Summit participants defined a rewarding environment as follows:

A rewarding USGS environment is one in which employees are motivated and energized to produce outstanding science and science support and are valued and recognized for their contributions.

This definition of Rewarding Environment goes beyond traditional notions of "rewards and recognition." Research on what employees find rewarding and motivating identifies a broad range of basic, intrinsic, extrinsic, and quality-of-worklife factors that drive employee performance, motivation, recruitment, and retention (Judge and others, 2001). Figure 2 summarizes the types of rewards that summit participants determined should be part of the USGS definition of a rewarding work environment.

Taking a more inclusive approach to a rewarding work environment offers many opportunities to affect employees' perceptions of the USGS as a rewarding place to work and to influence the *valued outcomes* that a rewarding work environment creates.

Conceptual Model of a Rewarding Environment

To enhance the understanding of a rewarding work environment at the USGS, a conceptual model of a rewarding work environment was developed. The USGS Rewarding Environment model is based upon an extensive body of existing organizational research on rewards, culture, and performance outcomes. (See appendix A.) The Rewarding Environment model includes the *key components* that are hypothesized to contribute to employees' perceptions of a rewarding work environment. The model

1. **Basic Workplace Rewards** – which are essential to an employee's security, safety, and success on the job
   - Pay and benefits
   - Clear performance expectations and feedback
   - Open communication
   - Effective leadership and management
   - A competent, committed, and caring supervisor
   - Respect and trust
   - Appropriate space, facilities, and equipment

2. **Intrinsic Rewards** – which give employees a personal sense of meaning and satisfaction in their work
   - Meaningful and challenging work
   - USGS stature and reputation
   - Quality colleagues
   - Professional development and skills enhancement
   - Personal fulfillment
   - Satisfaction in serving the public
   - Autonomy
   - Participation in decisionmaking

3. **Quality-of-Worklife Rewards** – which enable employees to manage their jobs and balance their worklives and homelives
   - Flexiplace and Alternative Work Schedules
   - Part-time work schedules and job sharing
   - Child care and elder care
   - Health and wellness programs and services
   - Employee Assistance Program and services
   - Fitness programs
   - Convenience services (such as store, automatic teller machine [ATM], snack bar)
   - Concierge services (such as dry cleaners, car wash)

4. **Extrinsic Rewards** – which come from others and range from simple expressions of appreciation to formal awards
   - Recognition for contributions
   - "Thank you" and other expressions of praise and appreciation
   - Non-monetary recognition
   - Length-of-service recognition
   - Monetary awards
   - Honor awards
   - Awards and recognition from external organizations

Figure 2.   Types of rewards in a rewarding work environment.

also identifies some of the individual and organizational *valued outcomes* that are hypothesized to result from having a Rewarding Environment culture. Figure 3 depicts the USGS Rewarding Environment model.

The *key components* that are hypothesized to affect perceptions of the USGS as a rewarding place to work include:

- USGS science vision

- Leadership and management practices

- The organization (including resources, operational support, and training)

- The work itself (the personal meaning of the work being done by the employee)

Each of these *key components* includes one or more elements that help define the component. The Rewarding Environment model postulates that these *key components* and the elements that define them have a direct impact on the following *valued outcomes* that the USGS is seeking:

- USGS science vitality

- Customer satisfaction with USGS products and services (as perceived by employees)

- Employee perceptions of the USGS as a rewarding place to work

- Heightened employee morale and commitment

- The ability to recruit and retain employees with critical skills

USGS Rewarding Environment Status Report

Because the Rewarding Environment model depicts the *key components* and *valued outcomes* of a Rewarding Environment culture, the model can serve as the framework for a Rewarding Environment status report for measuring and tracking USGS progress in creating a Rewarding Environment culture and achieving the *valued outcomes* the USGS is seeking. In this study, a baseline 2002 Rewarding Environment status report was created using employee responses to the 2002 OAS.

In creating the Rewarding Environment status report, each *key component* and *valued outcome* of the Rewarding Environment model was linked to one or more OAS questions. (See appendix B for the specific OAS questions used to measure each of the *key components* and *valued outcomes*.) For each *key component* and *valued outcome*, favorable employee responses to the corresponding OAS question(s) were averaged to determine a score, which was then expressed as a percentage of favorable (F) responses.[6] Figure 4 shows the 2002 USGS Rewarding Environment status report.

The following *key components* and *valued outcomes* were identified in the Rewarding Environment status report as rated **most favorably** by USGS employees.

Key components:
- Quality-of-worklife flexibility (78 percent F)
- The work itself (73 percent F)
- Resources (65 percent F)
- Managing diversity (64 percent F)
- Security and safety (63 percent F)

Valued outcomes:
- Employee perceptions of customer satisfaction (80 percent F)

- USGS as a rewarding place to work (63 percent F)

---

[6]"Favorable" responses include the "strongly agree" and "agree" responses to questions on the 2002 OAS. For purposes of the Rewarding Environment status report, results are presented as a percentage of favorable responses in order to facilitate: (1) comparison of favorable results among *key components* and *valued outcomes* and (2) tracking progress and improvement over time.

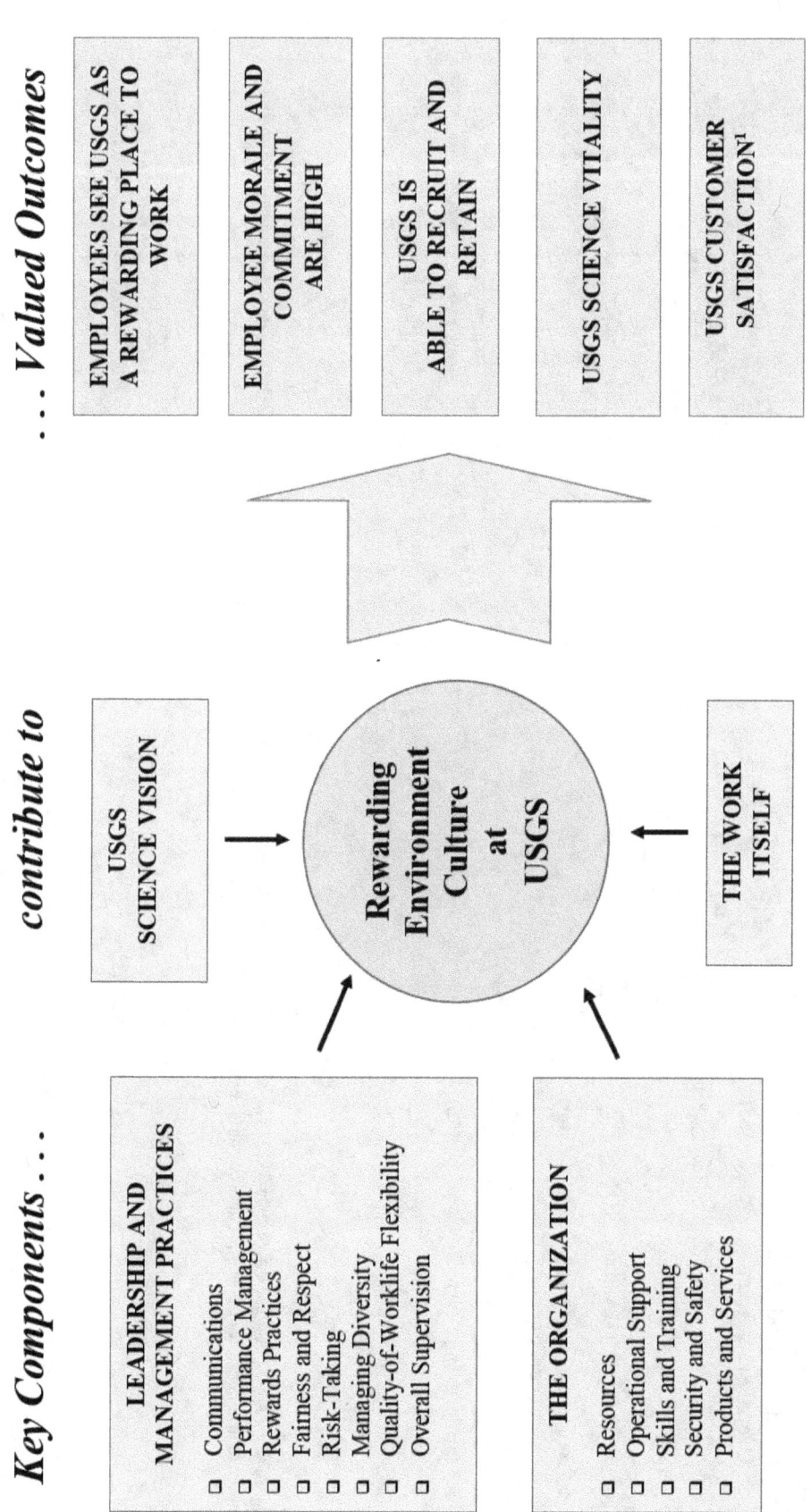

Figure 3.   Conceptual model of a rewarding work environment at the U.S. Geological Survey (USGS).

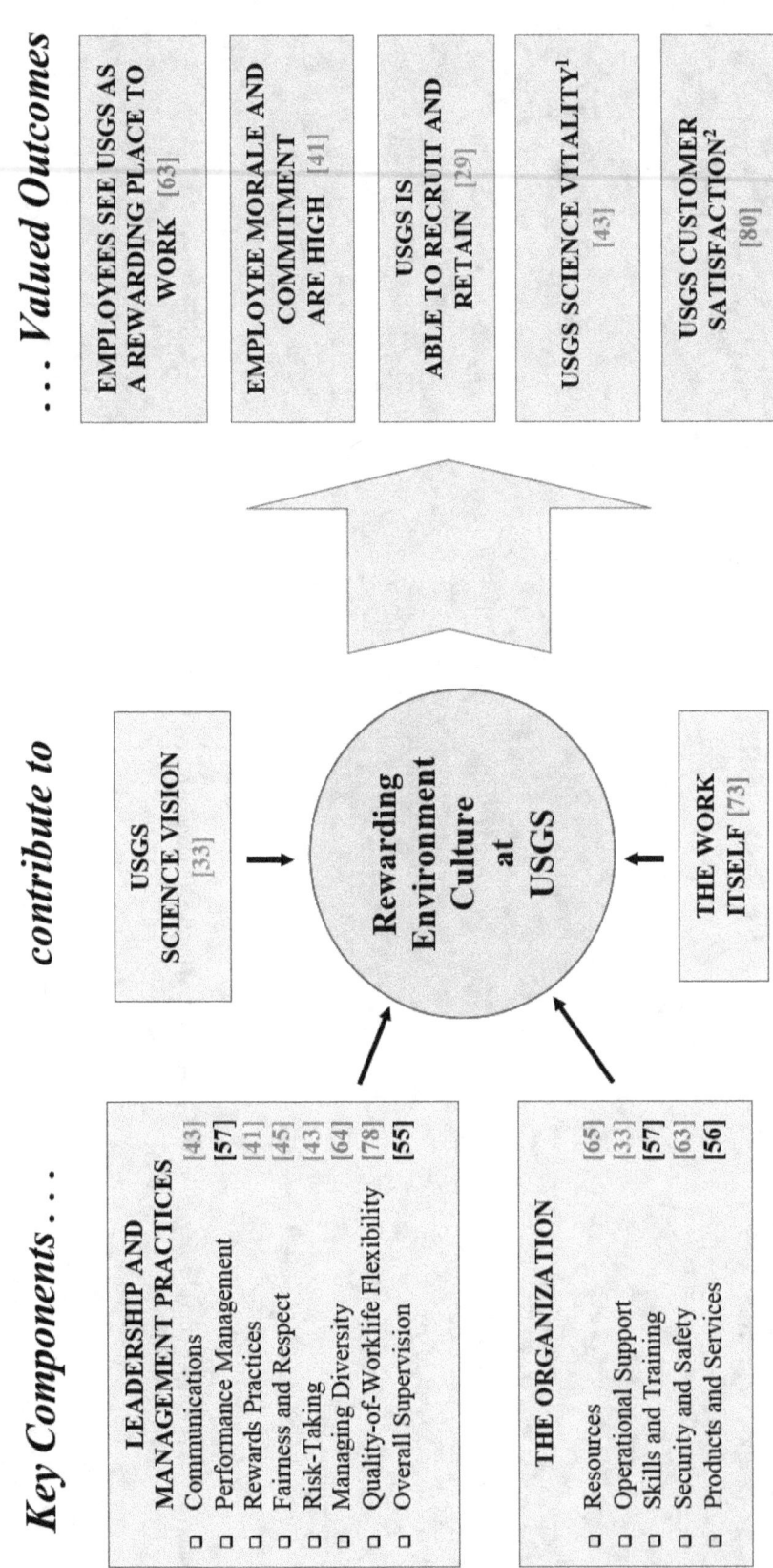

Figure 4. 2002 U.S. Geological Survey (USGS) Rewarding Environment status report. Favorable (F) percentage ratings on the 2002 Organizational Assessment Survey are shown in brackets: green = 60 percent or greater F, red = 45 percent or less F, and **black** = 46 to 59 percent F.

[1] As rated by research scientists
[2] Customer satisfaction rating as perceived by employees

Key Components . . .

contribute to

. . . Valued Outcomes

**LEADERSHIP AND
MANAGEMENT PRACTICES**
- Communications [43]
- Performance Management **[57]**
- Rewards Practices [41]
- Fairness and Respect [45]
- Risk-Taking [43]
- Managing Diversity [64]
- Quality-of-Worklife Flexibility [78]
- Overall Supervision **[55]**

THE ORGANIZATION
- Resources [65]
- Operational Support [33]
- Skills and Training **[57]**
- Security and Safety [63]
- Products and Services **[56]**

**USGS
SCIENCE VISION**
[33]

**THE WORK
ITSELF [73]**

Rewarding
Environment
Culture
at
USGS

**EMPLOYEES SEE USGS AS
A REWARDING PLACE TO
WORK** [63]

**EMPLOYEE MORALE AND
COMMITMENT
ARE HIGH** [41]

**USGS IS
ABLE TO RECRUIT AND
RETAIN** [29]

USGS SCIENCE VITALITY[1]
[43]

**USGS CUSTOMER
SATISFACTION**[2]
[80]

The following *key components* and *valued outcomes* were identified in the Rewarding Environment status report as rated **least favorably** by USGS employees.

Key components:
- Fairness and respect (45 percent F)
- Communications (43 percent F)
- Risk-taking (43 percent F)
- Rewards practices (41 percent F)
- USGS science vision (33 percent F)
- Operational support (33 percent F)

Valued outcomes:
- USGS science vitality as rated by research scientists (43 percent F)
- Employee morale and commitment (41 percent F)
- USGS ability to recruit and retain needed talent (29 percent F)

Summary of Findings From the 2002 Organizational Assessment Survey (OAS)

Whereas the Rewarding Environment status report uses the 2002 OAS results to provide a broad picture of USGS progress in creating a rewarding work environment, the OAS data themselves provide an in-depth look at rewards, recognition, and morale at the USGS. One of the six OAS topic areas addressed the question: "Is the USGS a Rewarding Place to Work?" Within that topic area, nine structured-response questions and one open-ended question dealt with employees' perceptions regarding rewards and recognition, including a question regarding the USGS as a rewarding place to work and a question related to morale at the employees' science center or office.

Employee Responses to OAS Questions on Rewards and Recognition

Table 1 shows employee responses to the nine structured-response OAS questions on rewards and recognition. The questions are grouped into those rated favorably by 60 percent or more of USGS employees (Rewarding Environment Strengths), those rated unfavorably by 30 percent or more (Rewarding Environment Weaknesses), and those that were rated as neither strengths nor weaknesses (Rewarding Environment Neutral).

In the area of rewards and recognition, employees identified the following as USGS **strengths**:

- An overall favorable impression of the USGS as a rewarding place to work

- Employees' conviction that the work they do contributes to the mission and accomplishments of the Bureau

- Employees' belief that their skills and abilities are being well utilized

Employees identified the following areas as **weaknesses**:

- The link between rewards and merit

- Recognition of employees for working together in cross-functional and cross-organizational teams

- Rewards practices

- Overall morale at the local science centers and offices

Employees rated the following areas as **neutral** (neither a strength nor a weakness):

- Feeling recognized and rewarded for their contributions to the USGS

- Being rewarded for providing high-quality products and services to their customers

These basic OAS findings indicate that while a majority of employees find the USGS to be a rewarding place to work overall, those perceptions are primarily related to employees' senses of meaning in the work they are doing and their personal satisfaction in how their skills and abilities are being utilized. While these factors are favorable contributors, they may not be enough to attract or retain talented employees who are offered the opportunity to apply their unique skills in another organization with an equally meaningful mission.

Table 1.   Summary of findings from the 2002 Organizational Assessment Survey (OAS) of the U.S. Geological Survey (USGS).

[The table summarizes by USGS regions and centers the Rewarding Environment strengths, neutrals, and weaknesses based on the 2002 OAS. Terms: %, percent; F, favorable; HQ, headquarters; RE, Rewarding Environment; UF, unfavorable]

Statement from the OAS	USGS overall	Eastern Region	Central Region	Western Region	National centers/HQ[1]	Bureau centers[2]
	%F / %UF	%F / %UF	%F / %UF	%F / %UF	%F / %UF	%F / %UF
RE Strengths (60 percent or more favorable)						
2. My job makes good use of my job-related skills and abilities.	71 / 16	71 / 16	73 / 14	73 / 14	70 / 18	72 / 19
6. In the work I do, I feel that I am directly contributing to the science mission and accomplishments of the Bureau.	79 / 8	80 / 12	78 / 8	82 / 7*	78 / 9	70 / 10*
8. Overall, I find the USGS a rewarding place to work.	63 / 16	60 / 18	63 / 16	67 / 13*	64 / 13	62 / 18
RE Neutral						
3. I feel recognized and rewarded for my contributions to the USGS.	48 / 29	44 / 32*	49 / 29	52 / 27*	48 / 26	57 / 24*
7. Employees are rewarded for providing high-quality products and services to their internal and/or external customers.	42 / 29	39 / 32	41 / 31	44 / 26	42 / 25	47 / 26
RE Weaknesses (30 percent or more unfavorable)						
1. Recognition and rewards are based on merit.	48 / 30	48 / 28	50 / 26	53 / 24*	49 / 25	53 / 25
4. Employees are recognized and rewarded for working together in teams and across functional or organizational boundaries.	34 / 36	33 / 36	35 / 36	32 / 36	32 / 35	44 / 33*
5. Employee contributions are recognized, communicated, and celebrated.	39 / 33	36 / 35	39 / 33	42 / 28	38 / 32	40 / 30
9. Overall, morale at my Science Center/Office is...[3]	23 / 39	21 / 44	24 / 39	27 / 35*	19 / 39*	28 / 35

Strengths and weaknesses are color coded to show overall patterns.

Strength (60 percent or more favorable)

Weakness (30 percent or more unfavorable)

[1] National centers/HQ includes offices of the Chief Scientists in Reston, Va., as well as national science centers.

[2] Bureau centers includes Office of the Director, as well as HQ functional offices such as Geographic Information Office (GIO), Administrative Policy and Services (APS), and Human Resources (HR).

[3] Statement 9 with responses was "Overall, morale at my Science Center/Office is very high, high, average, low, very low, don't know/not applicable."

* Statistically significant differences from USGS overall in percent F ($p \leq 0.05$) using z-test.

All of the areas identified as weaknesses or rated as neutral also are critical aspects of a rewarding work environment. These areas are related directly to the working environment established by managers and supervisors. Because these areas are under the direct control of supervisors and managers, they clearly are areas of opportunity for improving the work environment at the USGS and for strengthening the Bureau's ability to attract, retain, and motivate high performers.

Group Differences in Rewarding Environment Perceptions

In addition to employee responses at the Bureau level, the differences in employee perceptions by demographic groups (regions, disciplines, supervisory levels, grade levels, employment status, tenure, gender, age, disability, race, and ethnicity) also were examined. Table 1 shows regional differences in responses to the nine rewards and recognition questions and shows the pattern of strengths and weaknesses across the regions. For the most part, regional differences were small, although Western Region and Bureau centers tended to be slightly more favorable in some areas than the other regions.

Table 2 shows responses to the statement, "Overall, I find the USGS a rewarding place to work," for those demographic groups that showed meaningful differences from USGS overall results, highlighting differences with a magnitude of 10 percentage points higher or lower.

Again, the number of groups that showed meaningful differences from the USGS as a whole is relatively small. Executives and high-graded employees reported higher than average perceptions of Rewarding Environment, whereas wage-grade and some minority groups reported lower than average perceptions. Interestingly, young employees (under 30) and less tenured employees (2 years or less) also were higher in their ratings of the USGS as a rewarding place to work, whereas those with more tenure (11–20 years) were lower than average in their perceptions of the USGS as a rewarding place to work.

Employee Comments on Rewarding Environment

Table 3 summarizes the key themes in employees' written responses to the write-in question:

What is the ONE most important thing that managers and/or employees at your location could do to make the USGS a more rewarding place to work?

Of the 5,355 employees who responded to the OAS, nearly 2,500 responded to this write-in question. Employee responses (shown below in rank order, with representative employee comments) relate to the following three predominant themes.

1. **Managers' Rewards Practices**, including timing, timeliness, amount, and frequency of rewards (mentioned by 44 percent of respondents)

   - "Be continuous in recognition throughout the year (thank you and good job counts); too often August [end of performance appraisal period] is the time of monetary awards which are given to ALL (not just the high performers). So timing is off as well as application."

   - "Make rewards and recognition a public thing. It is now basically an underground system."

   - "Rewards and recognition are meaningless many times. In other words--it's OK to provide a poor work environment all year long, but oh--by the way--good job!?"

   - "Improve and increase the rewards to a more reasonable level and improve the timeliness of these rewards. Budgets are not large enough to reward in any meaningful way."

2. **Lack of Opportunities and Support** (mentioned by 34 percent of respondents)

   - "Management cannot seem to prioritize work or set policies. We are not a team. I don't get the overall administrative support from my direct line manager or from the USGS administration to do my job properly."

   - "Perform BASIC managerial duties. (Communication of goals/expectations, feedback on performance, completion of performance reviews, provide guidance or training to perform duties, etc.)

3. **Fairness and Respect** (mentioned by more than 11 percent of respondents)

   - "The most important thing in my particular office would be to act more fairly in the assignment of tasks and projects, because that is where the employee gets the experience needed to apply for promotional opportunities. The managers in my area mold the employees they are friends with by assigning specific projects and then making experience in those projects mandatory for the job opportunities."

- "Don't hand out awards to people for doing what is normal, everyday business for the rest of the staff. It's demeaning to those of us who put in extra hours routinely just to get the job done."

- "This center is great for awarding the supervisors who didn't do any work, just served as the figurehead and forgetting to award the technicians who actually did the work!"

Additional representative comments for each of the themes are provided in appendix C. Employees' written comments closely paralleled their answers to the structured-response questions. The issue of greatest concern to employees was managers' rewards practices, followed by concerns about opportunities and support, fairness and respect, communications, and overall supervision.

Hard Data on Awards and Employee-Initiated Separations

An outcome of the 2000 Rewards Summit was recognition of the need for hard data on Rewarding Environment to complement the OAS data. A comprehensive Rewarding Environment measurement plan was subsequently developed. (See appendix D for the Rewarding Environment measurement plan.)

For the 2002 baseline assessment of Rewarding Environment, hard data were gathered on the following measures:

- The amount and distribution of cash awards

- The use of Time Off Awards and Quality Step Increases (QSIs)

- Employee-initiated separations

Data on the above measures are summarized in table 4.

The data indicate that in the baseline year of 2002, the USGS gave:

- **6,584 cash awards.** These awards averaged $956 per award and represented a total expenditure of approximately 1.2 percent of total salary. The total number of cash awards divided by the total number of eligible employees and multiplied by 100 represents 57.6 percent of eligible employees.[7]

- **504 Time Off Awards.** The total number of Time Off Awards divided by the total number of eligible employees and multiplied by 100 represents 4.5 percent of eligible employees.

- **287 QSIs.** These QSIs represented 2.9 percent of eligible employees.

A review of the data indicates that there are substantial differences in rewards practices across regions, disciplines, and occupational groups. These differences may indicate the need for more guidance and dialogue among USGS leaders to improve equity and fairness of rewards practices across the USGS.

No substantial differences were found in employee-initiated separation data across regions, disciplines, or occupational groups. In fact, the voluntary separation rate for permanent employees is quite low overall (less than 5 percent) and does not appear to be a concern at the present time. These data bear watching in the future, however, as the percentage of employees covered by the portable Federal Employees' Retirement System increases. Retirement benefits may be a less compelling retention factor and other aspects of a rewarding work environment may play a more important role in recruiting and retaining employees.

---

[7]Federal Personnel Payroll System (FPPS) data provide only the total number of cash and Time Off Awards granted; FPPS cannot identify the number of awards given to individual employees. Thus, it is only possible to calculate the total number of cash and Time Off Awards as a percentage of eligible employees; it is not possible to calculate the percentage of eligible employees who actually received cash and Time Off Awards. It is possible to calculate the percentage of eligible employees who received a QSI, however, because an employee can receive only one QSI in a given year.

Table 2.   Summary of group differences in Rewarding Environment perceptions within the U.S. Geological Survey (USGS).

[The table shows employee responses by group to statement 8 in the 2002 Organizational Assessment Survey: "Overall, I find the USGS a rewarding place to work." Terms: %, percent; F, favorable; *n*, sample number; SES, employees of the Senior Executive Service; SL, senior level employees; ST, scientific or professional employees; UF, unfavorable]

Groups with Higher Favorable Rating than USGS Overall

Group	Subgroup	% F	% UF	Statistically significant*	*n*
USGS	USGS overall	63	16		5,319
Region	Western	67	13	Yes	1,103
Discipline	Human Resources	77	12	Yes	78
	Water	67	13	Yes	2,066
Supervisory level	Executive	79	10	Yes	48
Grade level	ST	79	21	No	14
	SES/SL	86	0	No	14
Employment status	Temporary employees	71	9	Yes	580
Tenure	Less than 2 years	76	10	Yes	483
Gender	Males	65	15	Yes	2,925
Age	Under 30	73	8	Yes	444
Race	White	65	15	Yes	4,186

Groups with Lower Favorable Rating than USGS Overall

Group	Subgroup	% F	% UF	Statistically significant*	*n*
USGS	USGS overall	63	16		5,319
Discipline	Geography	58	20	Yes	469
	Biology	55	20	Yes	850
Disabled	Yes	52	23	Yes	193
Grade level	Wage grade	51	30	No	37
Tenure	11-20 years	60	18	Yes	1,457
Race	American Indian/ Alaska Native	51	29	No	35
	Black or African American	54	24	Yes	112
	Other	55	21	Yes	217
Ethnicity	Hispanics	55	23	Yes	161

*Statistically significant differences from USGS overall in percent F ($p < 0.05$) using z-test.

With relatively large sample sizes, a small magnitude of difference can be statistically significant.

   More meaningful differences of 10 percentage points or more are highlighted:

   [ ]   10 percent or more **above** USGS overall; that is, ≥73 percent F

   [ ]   10 percent or more **below** USGS overall; that is, ≤53 percent F

Table 3.   Summary by theme of employee comments from the 2002 Organizational Assessment Survey of the U.S. Geological Survey (USGS).

[The table summarizes written responses to the question: "What is the ONE most important thing that managers and/or employees at your location could do to make the USGS a more rewarding place to work?" Terms: %, percent; HQ, headquarters; n, sample number]

Theme	USGS overall (n=2,448)	Eastern Region (n=741)	Central Region (n=685)	Western Region (n=544)	National centers/HQ[1] (n=319)	Bureau centers[2] (n=159)
Rewards practices Timeliness of awards, frequency of awards, other rewards practices	44%	47%	46%	36%	45%	45%
Opportunities and support Promotion and advancement opportunities, training, mentoring, lack of software/ equipment, supervisors that do not support their employees	34%	29%	34%	42%	24%	11%
Fairness and respect Fairness, respect, trust	11%	11%	9%	10%	14%	24%
Communications issues Listening, giving feedback, communication	5%	5%	4%	5%	5%	6%
Funding issues Not enough budget; award amounts	4%	4%	3%	3%	4%	3%
Reorganization issues Anything related to USGS reorganization	1%	0%	0%	1%	3%	1%
Flexiplace issues Flexiplace/telecommuting and/ or quality-of-worklife flexibilities	0%	1%	0%	0%	2%	3%
We already do a great job (No changes required)	2%	2%	2%	2%	2%	6%

[1]National centers/HQ includes offices of the Chief Scientists in Reston, Va., as well as national science centers.

[2]Bureau centers includes Office of the Director, as well as HQ functional offices such as Geographic Information Office (GIO), Administrative Policy and Services (APS), and Human Resources (HR).

Table 4. Regional, discipline, and occupational group comparisons between employee perceptions (2002 OAS) and 2002 USGS data on rewards granted and employee-initiated separations.

Regional Comparisons

[Terms: $, dollar; %, percent; HQ, headquarters; OAS, Organizational Assessment Survey; SCEPs, Student Career Employment Program participants; USGS, U.S. Geological Survey]

Data	USGS overall	Eastern Region	Central Region	Western Region	HQ
OAS (number of employees responding)	5,319	1,367	1,328	1,103	879
"Overall, I find the USGS a rewarding place to work." (% favorable)	63%	60%	63%	67%	64%
Cash awards					
Number as % of eligible employees	57.6%	50.5%	66.0%	48.4%	72.1%
Average $ amount	$956	$894	$689	$1,149	$1,279
% of salary $	1.2%	1.1%	1.0%	1.3%	1.6%
Other rewards					
Time off; Number as % of eligible employees	4.5%	4.4%	7.9%	2.5%	2.2%
Quality Step Increase; % of eligible employees	2.9%	3.4%	2.9%	2.7%	2.3%
Employee-initiated separations*					
Employee-initiated separations, excluding SCEPs; % of employees	1.07%	1.35%	0.93%	0.76%	1.15%

*Includes retirements.

Discipline Comparisons

[Terms: $, dollar; %, percent; APS, Administrative Policy and Services; DO, Director's Office; GIO, Geographic Information Office; OAS, Organizational Assessment Survey; ORS, Office of Regional Services; SCEPs, Student Career Employment Program participants; USGS, U.S. Geological Survey]

Data	USGS overall	APS/ORS	Biology	DO	GIO	Geology	Geography	Water
OAS (number of employees responding)	5,319	165	850	75	72	761	469	2,066
"Overall, I find the USGS a rewarding place to work" (% favorable)	63%	64%	55%	86%	64%	66%	58%	67%
Cash awards								
Number as % of eligible employees	57.6%	146.2%	41.3%	46.9%	85.9%	54.6%	57.1%	57.1%
Average $ amount	$956	$1,236	$1,114	$1,123	$1,780	$1,234	$686	$757
% of salary $	1.2%	3.4%	1.3%	1.1%	2.0%	1.1%	0.8%	1.0%
Other rewards								
Time off; Number as % of eligible employees	4.5%	2.9%	8.8%	1.5%	3.6%	0.5%	15.3%	2.1%
Quality Step Increase; % of eligible employees	2.9%	3.5%	3.0%	1.6%	1.6%	2.4%	1.6%	3.4%
Employee-initiated separations*								
Employee-initiated separations, excluding SCEPs (% of employees)	1.07%	0.82%	0.94%	1.54%	0.00%	0.73%	0.36%	1.47%

*Includes retirements.

Table 4.   Regional, discipline, and occupational group comparisons between employee perceptions (2002 OAS) and 2002 USGS data on rewards granted and employee-initiated separations.—Continued

Occupational Group Comparisons

[Terms: $, dollar; %, percent; N/A, not applicable; OAS, Organizational Assessment Survey; SCEPs, Student Career Employment Program participants; USGS, U.S. Geological Survey]

Data	USGS overall	Administrative/ clerical	Computer	Wage grade	Science	Science technicians
OAS (number of employees responding)	5,319	632	305	47	2,337	830
"Overall, I find the USGS a rewarding place to work" (% favorable)	63%	63%	58%	55%	65%	65%
Cash awards						
Number as % of eligible employees	57.6%	99.6%	68.3%	40.4%	47.1%	44.3%
Average $ amount	$956	$1,053	$1,056	$847	$1,080	$547
% of salary $	1.2%	2.5%	1.4%	0.9%	0.9%	0.9%
Other rewards						
Time off; Number as % of eligible employees	4.5%	5.3%	3.0%	2.5%	4.6%	4.6%
Quality Step Increase; % of eligible employees	2.9%	5.3%	2.2%	N/A	3.0%	1.5%
Employee-initiated separations*						
Employee-initiated separations, excluding SCEPs (% of employees)	1.07%	1.80%	0.49%	2.36%	0.72%	1.26%

*Includes retirements.

Relation Between OAS Results and USGS Data on Rewards Practices and Employee-Initiated Separations

In addition to the awards and employee-initiated separation data, table 4 also shows the corresponding OAS findings by region, discipline, and occupational group. Having both OAS and hard data on the *key components* and *valued outcomes* of a rewarding work environment allows comparisons of important relations among these data.

Unfortunately, there are too few data in the 2002 hard data to test whether, for example, higher average cash awards or greater frequency of awards has an impact on employees' perceptions of the USGS as a rewarding place to work. A more complete set of data, rewards-practice measures, and Rewarding Environment outcome measures is necessary in order to draw conclusions about the relations between rewards practices and employee perceptions regarding a rewarding work environment. Over time, more complete data, improved measures, and convergent validation of OAS results and hard data will strengthen the ability of the USGS to identify those aspects of a rewarding work environment that are most critical to employees and those measures that are most effective at capturing key outcomes that are most important to the USGS.

Rewarding Environment and the 2002 Federal Human Capital Survey

In mid-2002, the Office of Personnel Management conducted the Federal Human Capital Survey (FHCS)[8] to assess the conditions that characterize high-performance organizations. Results of the survey were used to measure overall employee satisfaction and rank the "Best Places to Work" in the Federal Government. The "Best Places to Work" rankings show how USGS responses compare to Department of the Interior (DOI) and Governmentwide responses on various aspects of the work and work environment. The FHCS report also provides an "80th percentile" score for each survey question, which represents a benchmark to which the USGS should aspire.

Based on the "Best Places to Work" analysis, DOI tied for 8th place among 28 agencies, and the USGS tied for 57th place among 115 sub-agencies. Overall, USGS employees reported slightly lower levels of workplace satisfaction than the DOI or Governmentwide average. The USGS rated lower than the DOI or Governmentwide average on 24 of the 41 questions related most directly to Rewarding Environment. (See appendix E for a summary of the "Best Places to Work" analysis.)

USGS employees reported the **greatest** satisfaction on survey questions/statements that dealt with the work itself: knowing that the work they do is important, knowing how their work relates to the USGS mission and goals, liking the kind of work they do, and getting a feeling of personal accomplishment from the work. In addition, the USGS ranked **higher** than the DOI average, the Governmentwide average, and the 80th percentile on the following two statements regarding their organization:

- "I recommend my organization as a good place to work."

- "How would you rate your organization to work for compared to other organizations?"

The USGS ranked **lower** than the DOI average, the Governmentwide average, and the 80th percentile in response to the question: "How would you rate your overall satisfaction in your organization at the present time?"

USGS employees reported the **least** satisfaction on survey questions that dealt with leadership and rewards practices, motivation and commitment, and the ability of their work unit to recruit people with the right skills. On these areas, the USGS also ranked **lower** than the DOI and (or) Governmentwide averages.

The results of the "Best Places to Work" analysis closely parallel those of both the Rewarding Environment status report and the 2002 OAS results on rewards and recognition:

- The Rewarding Environment status report and 2002 OAS results identified the work itself, an overall impression of the USGS as a rewarding place to work, and employees' convictions that the work they do contributes to the USGS mission as **favorably rated**, as did the "Best Places to Work" analysis.

- The Rewarding Environment status report and 2002 OAS results identified rewards practices, science leadership, employee morale and commitment, and the ability of the USGS to attract and retain employees with critical skills as **unfavorably rated**, as did the "Best Places to Work" report.

---

[8]A total of 189 Federal agencies and sub-agencies were included in the survey. Questionnaires were distributed to a stratified random sample of over 200,000 employees, with more than 100,000 employees responding. A total of 1,610 USGS employees were included in the survey, and 823 employees (51 percent) responded.

III. Does Having a Rewarding Environment Make a Difference?

To determine whether a rewarding work environment makes a difference, it was necessary to validate the Rewarding Environment model (described in section II) and determine whether the *key components* of a rewarding work environment do have an impact on employees' opinions about the *valued outcomes* the USGS is seeking:

- USGS science vitality

- Customer satisfaction with USGS products and services

- Employee perceptions of the USGS as a rewarding place to work

- Heightened employee morale and commitment

- The ability to recruit and retain employees with critical skills

Multiple regression analyses of 2002 OAS data were used to validate the conceptual model and to determine the degree to which the *key components* of the model help explain employees' overall perceptions of the USGS as a rewarding place to work and the other *valued outcomes*. (See description of research methodology in appendix A.) Results of these analyses did support the conclusion that the *key components* of a rewarding environment do contribute to employees' perceptions of the USGS as a rewarding place to work and do lead to the other *valued outcomes* of the Rewarding Environment initiative. Sixty-four (64) percent of the variance in employees' perceptions of the USGS as a rewarding place to work was explained by *key components* of the Rewarding Environment model. Figure 5 summarizes the results of the correlational and multiple regression analyses and shows the links between *key components* and *valued outcomes* of the Rewarding Environment model.

The *key components* of the Rewarding Environment model that had the greatest impact on employee perceptions of the USGS as a rewarding place to work are ranked below in their order of importance.

1. Rewards practices	6. Performance management
2. Fairness and respect	7. Communications
3. Risk-taking	8. Skills and training
4. The work itself	9. Resources
5. Overall supervision	10. Managing diversity

The *key components* identified as contributing to employee perceptions of Rewarding Environment also were found to contribute to other *valued outcomes* identified in the Rewarding Environment model (see fig. 5). Specifically, the *key components* in the model were able to account for 62 percent of the variability in perceptions regarding employee morale and commitment, 44 percent of the variability in perceptions regarding the ability of the USGS to recruit and retain employees with critical skills, 55 percent of the variability in perceptions of USGS science vitality, and 48 percent of the variability in employee perceptions regarding customer satisfaction.

Given that human opinions and perceptions can be difficult to explain and predict, the results shown in figure 5 demonstrate that the Rewarding Environment model has a high level of predictive ability for the *valued outcomes* examined in this study, based on the standards of social science research. (See appendix F for a summary of the direct correlations between OAS Rewarding Environment scales and these *valued outcomes*.)

Differences Between "High Rewarding Environment" and "Low Rewarding Environment" Science Centers and Offices

To examine differences in employee perceptions regarding a rewarding work environment among the USGS science centers and offices, these science centers and offices were rank ordered on the basis of their employees' average response to the OAS statement: "Overall, I find the USGS a rewarding place to work." The rank ordering was used to identify and profile the top 15 ("High Rewarding Environment") and bottom 15 ("Low Rewarding Environment") science centers and offices.[9] High-ranked and low-ranked science centers and offices were found to differ significantly on almost all of the *key components* and *valued out-*

---

[9]The average Rewarding Environment score was 87 percent for the "High Rewarding Environment" science centers and offices and 38 percent for the "Low Rewarding Environment" science centers and offices. The average number of employees in both the "high" and "low" science centers and offices was equivalent (average 20 employees per science center and office), with the exception of one large center (about 100 employees) in the "Low Rewarding Environment" group.

Key Components . . .   contribute to   . . . Valued Outcomes

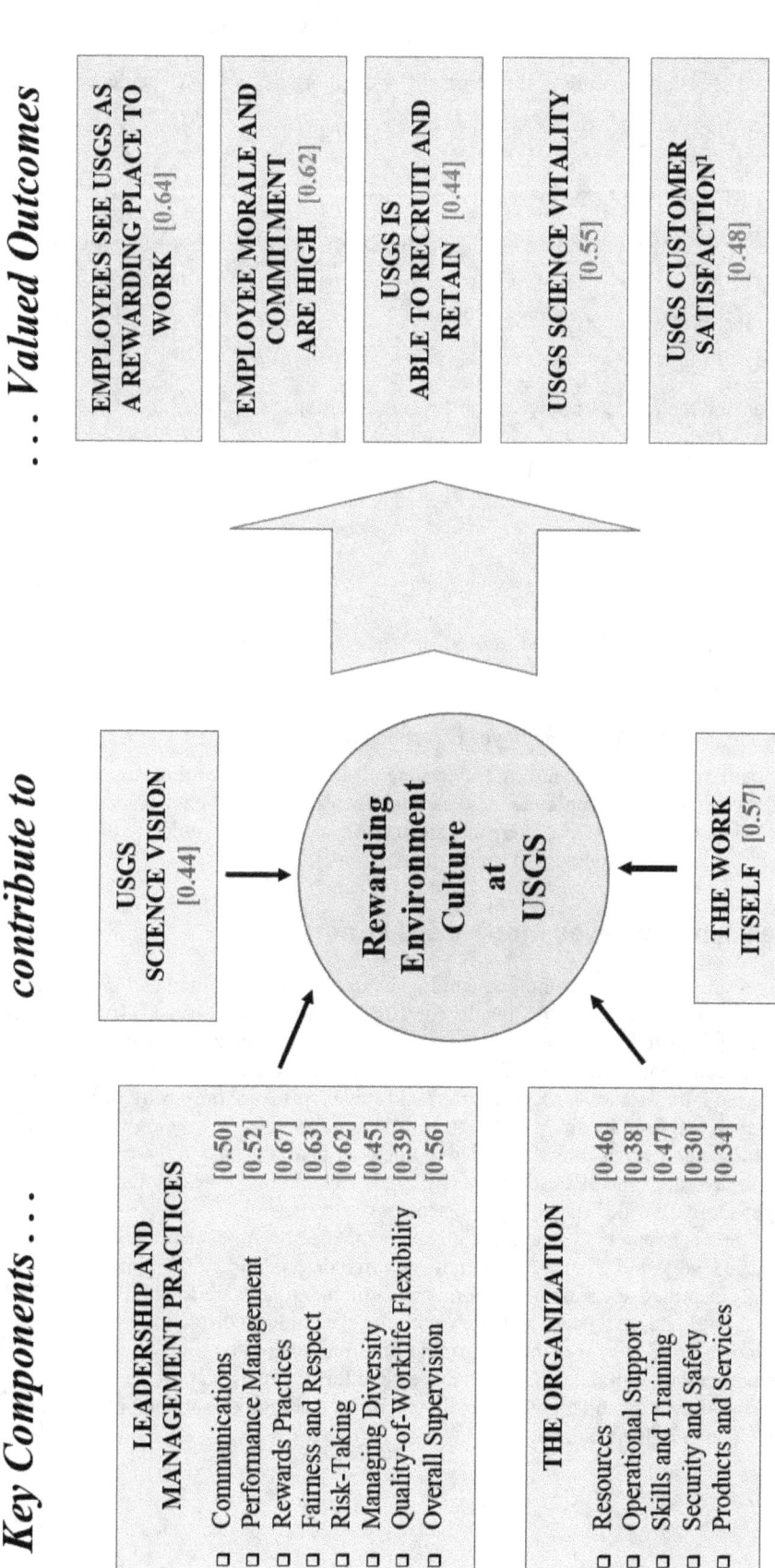

Leadership and Management Practices

☐ Communications [0.50]
☐ Performance Management [0.52]
☐ Rewards Practices [0.67]
☐ Fairness and Respect [0.63]
☐ Risk-Taking [0.62]
☐ Managing Diversity [0.45]
☐ Quality-of-Worklife Flexibility [0.39]
☐ Overall Supervision [0.56]

The Organization

☐ Resources [0.46]
☐ Operational Support [0.38]
☐ Skills and Training [0.47]
☐ Security and Safety [0.30]
☐ Products and Services [0.34]

USGS Science Vision [0.44]

Rewarding Environment Culture at USGS

The Work Itself [0.57]

Employees See USGS as a Rewarding Place to Work [0.64]

Employee Morale and Commitment Are High [0.62]

USGS is Able to Recruit and Retain [0.44]

USGS Science Vitality [0.55]

USGS Customer Satisfaction[1] [0.48]

[1]Customer satisfaction rating as perceived by employees

Figure 5. Results of analyses that answer the question, "Does a Rewarding Environment make a difference?" Numbers in blue reflect strength of correlation between this *key component* and employee responses to statement 8 on the Organizational Assessment Survey (OAS), "Overall, I find the USGS a rewarding place to work." Numbers in green reflect degree of variability in the *valued outcome* that is accounted for by the *key components* of a Rewarding Environment.

comes of a rewarding work environment. Table 5 summarizes the differences in responses from "High Rewarding Environment" and "Low Rewarding Environment" science centers and offices.

Science centers and offices that were ranked as "High Rewarding Environment" were more likely (by 25 percent or more) to have the following:

♦ Managers who—

- Create an environment that fosters and supports science excellence

- Focus on goals and objectives of the USGS and hold themselves and their employees accountable for achieving positive results

- Demonstrate fairness and respect, support risk-taking, and encourage others

- Collaborate and communicate effectively

- Provide employees the training they need and recognize employees for their contributions

♦ Workgroups that—

- Keep up with changing skill requirements

- Demonstrate flexibility in shifting resources as opportunities arise

"High Rewarding Environment" science centers and offices also were more likely (by 25 percent or more) to experience these *valued outcomes*:

- High ratings of the health and long-term viability of their science

- High levels of employee pride and commitment

- The ability to compete for and retain talent (as measured by employee perceptions)

The disparity between the 2002 OAS ratings of the "High Rewarding Environment" and "Low Rewarding Environment" science centers and offices indicates that (1) the behaviors that employees said created a rewarding work environment do lead to outcomes that the USGS values and (2) table 5 can be used by managers and supervisors as a practical guide to the types of actions that can and should be taken to enhance the work environment in their organizations.

The Links Among Rewarding Environment, Employee Morale, and Performance

Research indicates strong links among a rewarding work environment, employee morale, and individual and organizational performance (Judge and others, 2001). Analysis of the 2002 OAS results confirms a strong and expected relation between employee perceptions of the USGS as a rewarding place to work and employee morale and commitment at their own science center or office (fig. 5). Many of the same factors contributing to a rewarding work environment were also found to be related to employee perceptions of morale. (Responses to the fairness and respect questions and statements were the strongest predictors of morale and commitment.) Interestingly, while the OAS found a direct and high correlation between a rewarding work environment and morale, a rewarding work environment generally was rated favorably (63 percent favorable and 16 percent unfavorable), whereas morale was rated low (41 percent favorable and 39 percent unfavorable). This finding indicates that perceptions of a rewarding work environment and employee morale, while related, are two separate outcomes.

Although not directly tested in this study, there is strong evidence in the literature that demonstrates the relation between employee satisfaction and individual performance (Judge and others, 2001). In its research on predictors of employee performance, the Corporate Leadership Council (2002) identified seven "high-performance attitudes" that were found to predict high employee performance. Table 6 summarizes these attitudes. All seven attitudes, with the exception of discretionary effort, are included to some degree in the contributing factors (or outcomes) in the Rewarding Environment model.

The relations among a rewarding work environment, morale, and performance need further investigation. A rewarding work environment, high employee morale, and superior individual and organizational performance are important outcomes for the USGS, and it is essential to understand the factors that influence them.

Table 5. What contributes most to employee perceptions that the U.S. Geological Survey (USGS) is a rewarding place to work?

[The table summarizes differences in the percentage of favorable Organizational Assessment Survey (OAS) responses for high and low Rewarding Environment (RE) science centers and offices. Numbered statements and questions in this table correspond to the numbered statements and questions on the 2002 OAS (appendix B)]

OAS criterion statement	Percent favorable[1]	
	High RE[2]	Low RE[3]
8. Overall, I find the USGS a rewarding place to work.	87	38
Outcomes	**High RE**	**Low RE**
14. Employees at my science center/office take pride in being part of the USGS and are strongly committed to the Bureau's mission.	80	37
64. Considering its talent base, its science programs, and its science infrastructure, the USGS rates high in health and long-term viability as a scientific organization.	70	38
65. Overall, the USGS does a good job of staying relevant but neutral regarding public policy science issues.	87	55
66. The internal report review and approval process assures that USGS reports are accurate and unbiased and give proper credit to those who did the work.	81	45
71. My science center/office is able to compete for and retain the talent it needs in today's marketplace.	46	12
Leadership and management practices: Rewards practices	**High RE**	**Low RE**
3. I feel recognized and rewarded for my contributions to USGS.	64	31
4. Employees are recognized and rewarded for working together in teams and across functional or organizational boundaries.	49	24
5. Employee contributions are recognized, communicated, and celebrated.	58	26
7. Employees are rewarded for providing high-quality products and services to their internal and/or external customers.	59	30
Leadership and management practices: Fairness and respect	**High RE**	**Low RE**
1. Recognition and rewards are based on merit.	66	35
19a. How effective is management at your science center/office with these leadership behaviors: respecting others?	75	34
19e. How effective is management at your science center/office with these leadership behaviors: encouraging others?	63	25
36. In my science center/office, resources (people, funding) are generally allocated fairly and equitably.	57	25
Leadership and management practices: Risk-taking	**High RE**	**Low RE**
15. Employees are encouraged to ask questions and seek out the information they need to do their jobs.	82	45
17. The USGS values leadership.	58	27
27. Creativity and innovation are encouraged and rewarded.	63	31
72. My science center/office is flexible enough to shift resources to respond to new opportunities or challenges when they arise.	65	34
Leadership and management practices: Overall supervision	**High RE**	**Low RE**
19f. How effective is management at your science center/office with these leadership behaviors: focusing on the goals and objectives of the USGS?	79	36
19g. How effective is management at your science center/office with these leadership behaviors: collaborating?	64	28
21. Management in my science center/office is creating an environment that fosters and supports science excellence.	75	30

Table 5.   What contributes most to employee perceptions that the U.S. Geological Survey (USGS) is a rewarding place to work?—Continued

[The table summarizes differences in the percentage of favorable Organizational Assessment Survey (OAS) responses for high and low Rewarding Environment (RE) science centers and offices. Numbered statements and questions in this table correspond to the numbered statements and questions on the 2002 OAS (appendix B)]

	Percent favorable[1]	
Leadership and management practices: Performance management	**High RE[2]**	**Low RE[3]**
19b. How effective is management at your science center/office with these leadership behaviors: being and holding others accountable?	49	20
22. Employees are held accountable for achieving positive results.	67	33
Leadership and management practices: Communications	**High RE**	**Low RE**
12. Employees are kept informed on issues affecting their jobs.	60	31
19c. How effective is management at your science center/office with these leadership behaviors: communicating?	55	22
Skills/Training	**High RE**	**Low RE**
68. Employees receive the training they need to perform their jobs (for example, on-the-job training, conferences, workshops, coaching/mentoring).	75	40
69. My workgroup is keeping up with the changing skills required to do our jobs.	75	44
70. My supervisor puts a priority on making training and development opportunities available to employees.	67	35
Leadership and management practices: Managing diversity	**High RE**	**Low RE**
19d. How effective is management at your science center/office with these leadership behaviors: valuing differences?	61	30

[1]Questions shown are those on which there is a difference of 25 percentage points or more between high and low RE science centers and offices.

[2]High RE=average percentage favorable for top 15 science centers and offices on OAS statement 8: "Overall, I find the USGS a rewarding place to work."

[3]Low RE=average percentage favorable for bottom 15 science centers and offices on OAS statement 8.

Table 6.   Attitudes that contribute to high performance (from Corporate Leadership Council, 2002).

[The table provides definitions of high-performance attitudes]

High-performance attitude	Definition
Discretionary effort	• Extent to which employees put their full effort into their job, are constantly looking for ways to do their job better, are willing to put in the extra effort to get a job done when necessary, and believe that people would describe them as enthusiastic about the work they do
Organizational commitment	• Extent to which employees feel a strong sense of belonging to the organization, feel that the organization has a great deal of personal meaning for them, enjoy discussing the organization with people outside of it, and feel that the organization's problems are their own
Match with job	• Extent to which employees feel that their work is the right type of work for them and they are the right type of person for the job
Having necessary resources	• Extent to which employees think that they can always find out what they need to know to do their job successfully, always have the tools, resources, and technology they need to succeed at work, and know that they have the skills and knowledge to accomplish whatever it is that is asked of them at work
Team strength	• Extent to which employees believe that every person they work with brings something important to the team, all of the people they work with do their fair share of work, and everyone at work cares about whether they do a good job or not
Job satisfaction	• Extent to which employees describe themselves as very satisfied with their job and with the kind of work that they do
Intent to leave	• Extent to which employees do not intend to look for a new job with another organization in the next year, do not frequently think about quitting their job and leaving the organization, are not actively looking for a job with another organization, and have not made phone calls or sent out their résumé in order to find a job at another organization • Whether employees say that they would be happy to spend the rest of their career at their organization • Whether employees believe they could easily find a job at another organization

IV. USGS Rewarding Environment Successes and Challenges

Creating a rewarding work environment is a culture change that requires new ways of thinking and acting and innovative ways of motivating and recognizing employees. As part of assessing the Rewarding Environment culture change in the USGS, anecdotal information was gathered concerning the creative actions that are being taken in individual science centers and offices to enhance the work environment. Because many challenges remain in creating a Rewarding Environment culture, information was also gathered regarding the implementation challenges that must be addressed.

Success Stories From Across the USGS

Feedback from science centers and offices across the USGS indicates that many creative actions are being taken to bring about the Rewarding Environment culture change. A great deal of credit for the Rewarding Environment successes achieved to date goes to the managers, supervisors, and employees who have developed these innovative approaches. Examples of the types of actions being taken include the following:

Enhancing Communication

- **Face time**. Eastern Region (ER) Geography provides opportunities for employees to meet with the Regional Executive (REx) one on one. The REx also spends a few hours each week visiting with staff members at their worksites to see how people are doing. Results? Employees are provided opportunities to talk about their work, offer their ideas, and share their complaints and concerns.

- **Idea generation.** ER Geology uses Idea Generation Workshops with field trips to promote learning and knowledge exchange.

- **OAS results.** OAS results have been used by numerous managers as the basis for discussions on employee issues. ER has incorporated OAS results into its annual and strategic reviews to address specific employee issues.

Promoting Employee Career Development

- **Training.** The New Hampshire/Vermont Water Science Center has a policy that any employee can receive 1 week of appropriate, job-related training paid for out of the science center's overhead.

- **In-house classes.** ER Geography has organized several in-house training classes in which managers provide or participate in the classes. Results? Employees were impressed that managers would spend time with employees while they learned new skills.

Recognizing Peers

- **OCRS Stars award.** The Office of Central Regional Support (OCRS) created the "OCRS Stars" award. The OCRS purchased four star-shaped paperweights inscribed with "OCRS Star." Each was given to an outstanding employee with the instructions to pass it on to another OCRS employee in a public forum. Results? Employees enjoy having an opportunity to recognize their coworkers in this way.

- **USGS leadership coins.** Graduates of the USGS leadership courses receive a leadership coin and are asked to pass it on to other USGS employees when they witness an act of true leadership.

Helping Employees Balance Personal and Professional Demands

- **Convenience services.** The Earth Resources Observation and Science (EROS) Center has installed automated teller machines and stamp machines for staff convenience and established a Van Pool Association to assist employees with commuting arrangements.

- **Relocation.** The San Francisco Bay area had become cost prohibitive for some support employees to live, attrition was very high, and recruitment was a problem. The Western Office of Regional Support (ORS) decided to relocate the regional support staff to Sacramento. After 4 years, half of the 80 positions were located in Sacramento. This relocation has all been done on an optional basis without forcing any employee to relocate. Results? Although the original announcement was met with fear and anxiety by some employees, the relocation actually helped create a Rewarding Environment. Attrition is down, several employees are now first-time homeowners, ORS has moved into a permanent facility at California State University, Sacramento, and employee excitement and morale are up.

Creating Innovative Recognition

- **Innovation Award.** The Washington Water Science Center created an Innovation Award to recognize employees whose efforts in the areas of developing new technology, ideas, or creative applications are above and beyond the normal scope of their job. The award consists of $1,000 and the employee's name engraved on a permanent office plaque. The funds for the award are paid from the science center overhead account. Results? The award offers a means to recognize employees whose creativity is making a difference.

- **Rewards wall.** The EROS Center has created a rewards wall in its lobby where plaques and certificates received by employees are displayed.

- **Annual awards.** The Kansas Water Science Center has created annual awards in areas related to science where the science center wants to improve and lead the region, such as media exposure and scientific production. Results? The Kansas Water Science Center leads the Central Region in these two areas.

Fostering Esprit de Corps

- **Hydrotones.** The Hydrotones (Washington Water Science Center's own singing group) have special center carols, in which the Hydrotones spoof events that have happened in the center over the past year. Results? Center employees have fun, create and honor traditions, and build a sense of belonging to the USGS and the center.

- **Office photo album.** The Office of the Northeastern Regional Hydrologist has created an office photo album capturing important events that are meaningful to region personnel. Results? Employees have created a running history of the office–the region's story in pictures.

These and other "Best Practices from Across the USGS" can be found on the Rewarding Environment Web site, an internal USGS site. These examples are essential reading for all managers, supervisors, and employees interested in creating a more rewarding work environment.

Implementation Challenges

The preceding success stories demonstrate that progress is being made in creating a Rewarding Environment culture. As with all culture change, however, there are implementation challenges that must be addressed. Experience in implementing the Rewarding Environment culture change has identified the following challenges.

- **Maintaining managers' focus.** Creating a rewarding environment is a culture change, and culture change takes time. For many managers, maintaining focus on long-term change is difficult in the face of pressing programmatic, business, and budget issues.

- **Combating cynicism and skepticism.** Some employees and supervisors have stated that it is disingenuous to talk about creating a rewarding work environment in the midst of concerns about terrorism, budget cuts, possible downsizing, and competitive sourcing.

- **Communicating the science outcomes of a rewarding work environment.** Many supervisors and managers view creating a rewarding work environment as a "feel good" effort rather than a business strategy to invest in their people and their science.

- **Obtaining accurate, reliable, and easily retrievable data.** Data needed to assess progress in implementing the Rewarding Environment culture change (for example, acceptance rates for USGS positions) either are not available or are not available in an automated form that is easily retrieved.

In addition, the following cultural issues identified by employees in the 2002 OAS are barriers to culture change that must be overcome if the USGS is to succeed in creating and sustaining a rewarding work environment.

- **Communication.** Employees said that they are not kept informed of issues affecting their jobs; the science goals and vision have not been effectively communicated to them; job expectations have not been made clear; and managers are not good at listening to their employees or involving them in the decisionmaking process.

- **Risk-taking.** Employees said that risk-taking is not encouraged without fear of punishment for mistakes. Risk-taking is critical to culture change, which mandates new behaviors. Managers must be supportive of and recognize those who are willing to take the risk of demonstrating the desired new behaviors.

- **Accepting accountability.** Employees do not see managers, supervisors, and employees holding themselves and others accountable for their performance and actions. Accountability is defined as following through on commitments, admitting mistakes, rewarding those who are successful, and effectively dealing with employees who are poor performers. Accountability has a substantial impact on employee morale and the work environment in general.

- **Managing people.** Employees said that many managers know how to manage science projects but not people. Until managing people becomes a priority for the USGS and its managers, communication, risk-taking, and accountability will continue to be issues. This problem is exacerbated by the fact that supervisory and managerial training in the USGS is limited; there are few feedback mechanisms in place to evaluate managerial and supervisory performance adequately; and there are no standardized processes for assessing the competencies of managers and supervisors either before they are placed in supervisory or managerial positions or afterwards.

V. Conclusions and Implications for Rewarding Environment Culture Change

The findings of this study of Rewarding Environment at the USGS, the factors that contribute to it, and the outcomes that flow from it help provide direction and insight into the nature and focus for continued Rewarding Environment culture change activities. The preliminary Rewarding Environment conceptual model, developed and tested using 2002 OAS data, was used to identify those aspects of the culture that contribute directly to employees' perceptions of the USGS as a rewarding place to work. Research results also indicate the impact these factors have on important outcomes at the individual, science center, and Bureau levels.

Specific conclusions from this study as they relate to Rewarding Environment culture change include the following:

1. The USGS has taken a comprehensive, systematic and well-thought-out approach to changing its Rewarding Environment culture. The USGS has invested substantial time and effort in attempting to bring about and support a Rewarding Environment culture, and has been persistent in its efforts.

2. As a result of a sustained effort in the area of Rewarding Environment, the USGS has achieved numerous successes that demonstrate the ability of USGS managers and supervisors to be effective in creating a rewarding workplace. At the same time, many challenges and barriers to a rewarding work environment continue to exist. These challenges and barriers have direct implications for the continued implementation of the Rewarding Environment effort.

3. The Rewarding Environment culture at the USGS has both strengths and weaknesses (table 1). While a majority of employees find the USGS a rewarding place to work overall, that perception seems to be based heavily on the sense of personal contribution to the mission and the satisfaction that employees see in the work itself. Employees seem to find the ways in which managers deal with rewards and recognition far from rewarding, and employees describe overall morale at the USGS as low.

4. Nine of the ten factors that were found to contribute to a Rewarding Environment culture have to do with how individuals are managed (fig. 5). Write-in comments on the 2002 OAS indicate that the availability of development and advancement opportunities and managerial support also are key factors in a Rewarding Environment culture.

5. Overall, there are many similarities in the Rewarding Environment culture across the Bureau (tables 1, 2). Important differences, however, were found in perceptions of Rewarding Environment by grade level, by discipline, and for minority groups, which indicates the need to examine further the consistency and fairness of rewards practices.

6. Despite similarities in the Rewarding Environment profiles across the Bureau, there are clear differences between "High Rewarding Environment" and "Low Rewarding Environment" science centers and offices (table 5). The study results support the conclusion that these differences in Rewarding Environment culture do make a difference in *valued outcomes* of importance to employees and the organization. The study results also identify some specific actions that can be taken to create a rewarding work environment.

7. Meaningful differences were found in rewards practices related to the use of cash and other awards (table 4; appendix D). These differences speak to the need for guidance that will enhance consistency and cross-organizational fairness.

8. The USGS has had many successes in implementing a Rewarding Environment culture and should be able to capitalize on the lessons learned and on the interest and momentum that have begun to build for creating a Rewarding Environment culture at the USGS (section IV).

Priorities for Action

Together, the results of the Rewarding Environment status report (fig. 4) and the multiple regression analyses showing the impact of the *key components* of a Rewarding Environment on USGS *valued outcomes* (fig. 5) provide information that can be used to identify priority actions for enhancing the Rewarding Environment culture at the USGS.

Figure 6 shows a Rewarding Environment priority matrix, which plots these two factors—employee perceptions of the *key components* of a rewarding work environment and the impact that those components have in achieving USGS *valued outcomes*. The priority matrix ranks the *key components* of a Rewarding Environment and places them in one of four quadrants based on their score on the Rewarding Environment status report (fig. 4) and their impact on USGS *valued outcomes* (fig. 5).

The lower right quadrant, labeled **Top Priority**, contains the low-scoring, high-impact components. These are the areas that are most in need of improvement and that, if improved, would have the greatest relative impact on the overall levels of employee perceptions of the Rewarding Environment culture at the USGS. Components that fall into this "Top Priority" quadrant are, in priority order, rewards practices, fairness and respect, risk-taking, overall supervision, performance management, communications, skills and training, and science vision.

The upper right quadrant, labeled **Build On**, contains the high-scoring, high-impact components. These are areas where the USGS is relatively successful, but where progress must continue to be made because of the high impact that these components have on the Rewarding Environment culture. Components that fall into the "Build On" quadrant include the work itself, resources, and managing diversity.

The upper left quadrant, labeled **Maintain**, contains the high-scoring, low-impact components. These are areas where the USGS is relatively successful and where progress should be maintained even though the impact of these areas on the Rewarding Environment culture is lower than that of the high-impact components. Components that fall into the "Maintain" quadrant include quality-of-worklife flexibility and security and safety.

The lower left quadrant, labeled **Monitor**, contains the low-scoring, low-impact components. These are areas that are in need of improvement but that should just be watched for any change because they have a lower impact on a rewarding work environment. Components that fall into the "Monitor" category include products and services and operational support.

Implications for Leadership of Rewarding Environment Culture Change Effort

The USGS has made substantial progress in its Rewarding Environment culture change effort, although much remains to be done (fig. 1). Rewarding Environment has been successfully defined and shown to be an important contributor to *valued outcomes* for the USGS. Progress has been made in "getting the word out" through a Rewarding Environment Handbook, training, and an internal USGS Web site. A limited communications plan has ensured that employees have received key messages about the USGS commitment to a rewarding work environment, and a feedback loop with employees has been created by using the OAS as a key measure of success.

In order to fully integrate Rewarding Environment practices into the USGS culture, the key constituent groups who have been leading this effort must continue to play different and complementary roles in carrying the Rewarding Environment effort forward. Accountability for implementing Rewarding Environment practices must be placed on the shoulders of line managers and supervisors, with support and reinforcement from USGS senior leaders. The Rewarding Environment Program Manager should shift the focus toward providing the measures and tools necessary to support the USGS Rewarding Environment strategy and ensuring that Rewarding Environment is incorporated into related human capital management programs and initiatives and that appropriate linkages to Rewarding Environment are made.

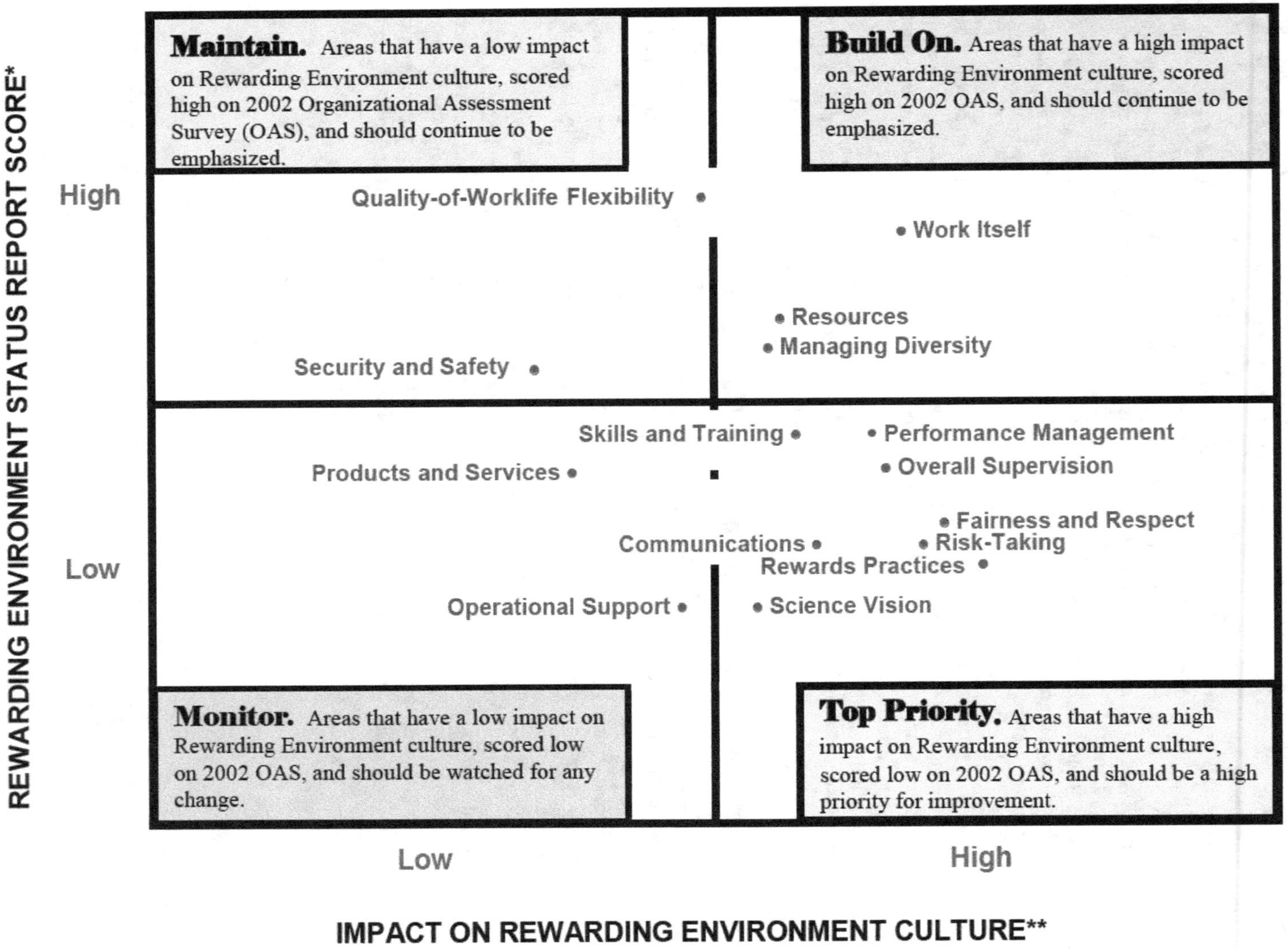

Maintain. Areas that have a low impact on Rewarding Environment culture, scored high on 2002 Organizational Assessment Survey (OAS), and should continue to be emphasized.

Build On. Areas that have a high impact on Rewarding Environment culture, scored high on 2002 OAS, and should continue to be emphasized.

Monitor. Areas that have a low impact on Rewarding Environment culture, scored low on 2002 OAS, and should be watched for any change.

Top Priority. Areas that have a high impact on Rewarding Environment culture, scored low on 2002 OAS, and should be a high priority for improvement.

- Work Itself
- Resources
- Managing Diversity
- Performance Management
- Overall Supervision
- Fairness and Respect
- Risk-Taking
- Communications
- Rewards Practices
- Science Vision
- Quality-of-Worklife Flexibility
- Security and Safety
- Skills and Training
- Products and Services
- Operational Support

REWARDING ENVIRONMENT STATUS REPORT SCORE*

High   Low

IMPACT ON REWARDING ENVIRONMENT CULTURE**

Low   High

*Based on status report results (fig. 4). High = rated 60 percent or higher on 2002 Organizational Assessment Survey (OAS). Low = rated 45 percent or lower on 2002 OAS.

**Based on scale correlations with OAS statement 8: "Overall, I find the USGS a rewarding place to work" (fig. 5). High = 40 percent or higher correlation. Low = 39 percent or lower correlation.

Figure 6. The Rewarding Environment priority matrix, which can be used to determine those areas requiring action.

VI. Recommendations for Enhancing USGS Rewarding Environment Efforts

In recognition of the differing and evolving roles of the various constituent groups having an accountability for creating a Rewarding Environment culture at the USGS, recommendations are offered for managers and supervisors, the Rewarding Environment Program Manager, and USGS senior leaders.

Actions Managers and Supervisors Can Take To Enhance the Rewarding Environment Culture in Their Centers

1. **Learn about rewarding environment.** Managers and supervisors should become familiar with USGS work on creating a rewarding work environment and look for ways to link Rewarding Environment practices to the outcomes that are important to their science center, program, or office. Managers and supervisors should read the Rewarding Environment Handbook, become familiar with findings from the USGS study on the subject, enroll in one of the supervisory or leadership courses that address this topic, and contact their servicing Human Resources (HR) Office or the Rewarding Environment Program Manager, who can suggest other resources to explore.

2. **Use and support the Organizational Assessment Survey (OAS).** Managers and supervisors should encourage employees to participate in the next OAS. Managers and supervisors need to let employees know (1) that the OAS is important to employees and to the USGS and (2) that they are open to feedback and willing to listen. Managers and supervisors should make a commitment to employees—and follow through on that commitment—to work together to make changes to improve the work environment and the organization. Managers and supervisors should review the 2002 OAS Results Report for their science center or office, compare these results to those of the High and Low Rewarding Environment science centers and offices (table 5), and use the priority matrix (fig. 6) to plot their own OAS results. Managers and supervisors should use this analysis to understand their organizations and identify where progress has or has not been made as a means of preparing for the next OAS. If help is needed in planning, strategizing, or taking action, managers and supervisors should contact the Rewarding Environment Program Manager, the Employee Survey Program Manager, or their servicing HR Office.

3. **Do a self-assessment.** Managers and supervisors should complete a self-assessment to see how many of the types of rewards identified in this report and in the Rewarding Environment Handbook are in use on a regular basis in their science center or office. Managers and supervisors should try creative and inexpensive new ways to reward employees and enhance the work environment.

4. **Ask employees what they value.** Managers and supervisors should incorporate a discussion of Rewarding Environment in midyear progress reviews and the end-of-year performance appraisal discussion with employees. Managers and supervisors should use the questionnaires in the Rewarding Environment Handbook as a basis for talking with employees, individually or in a team meeting, about what motivates employees, what rewards they value most, and what can be done to let employees know how much they are appreciated and valued.

5. **Understand the culture.** Managers and supervisors should use the Rewarding Environment priority matrix (fig. 6) to understand which aspects of the work environment have the greatest impact on the Rewarding Environment culture in their science center, office, or team and should focus their efforts on building a Rewarding Environment culture in those areas.

6. **Read and use success stories.** Managers and supervisors should read the Rewarding Environment success stories on the internal USGS Rewarding Environment Best Practices Web site. Points of contact are identified and can be consulted to obtain additional information on intriguing ideas. Successful approaches that others have taken can be adopted or can be tailored to fit the needs and preferences of the science center, office, or team.

7. **Share success stories.** Managers and supervisors should share their success stories (past or present) by adding them to the USGS Rewarding Environment Best Practices Web site. Names and office telephone numbers should be included so that other managers and supervisors can call for additional information.

8. **Interview prospective supervisors.** Managers and supervisors should ask applicants for supervisory positions: "If you were selected for this position, what would you do to create a rewarding work environment for your group?" and "What have you done in the past to create a rewarding work environment?"

9. **Model Rewarding Environment actions and behaviors.** Managers and supervisors should demonstrate fairness and respect when dealing with all employees, ensure that employees understand how meaningful their work is, trust employees to take risks, and be sure that their basic supervisory needs are being met.

10. **Spread the word.** Managers and supervisors should make recognition a regular part of staff meetings, publicize the actions being taken to enhance the work environment, and coach and support other managers and supervisors in becoming more effective at creating a Rewarding Environment culture.

Actions the Rewarding Environment Program Manager Can Take To Improve the Impact of the Rewarding Environment Culture Change Effort

1. **Enhance management support.** The Rewarding Environment Program Manager should identify a new organizational champion to support the Rewarding Environment initiative and identify senior and middle managers throughout the organization who can serve as Rewarding Environment leaders and role models. Maintaining a clear connection to senior leaders in the organization is critical to ensuring the continued legitimacy and support for this effort.

2. **Develop a Rewarding Environment network.** The Rewarding Environment Program Manager should develop a network of Bureau, regional, and local Rewarding Environment champions and servicing HR specialists to help guide and support implementation activities in the field and at headquarters. The Rewarding Environment Program Manager should capitalize on the learning and enthusiasm of Leadership 101 and 201 classes by challenging participants to be part of the Rewarding Environment network. These additional resources are needed to help ensure that the Rewarding Environment culture change efforts are translated into management practices at the local level.

3. **Update goals and objectives.** The Rewarding Environment Program Manager should review and update the Rewarding Environment vision, goals, objectives, and implementation plans to ensure continued alignment with new strategic developments and directions of relevance to the USGS and with the successes and impact of the Rewarding Environment culture change effort.

4. **Identify and address barriers.** The Rewarding Environment Program Manager should understand the barriers to creating a Rewarding Environment culture at the individual, local, and organizational levels in order to better focus training and other implementation activities.

5. **Refine Rewarding Environment measurement.** The Rewarding Environment Program Manager should continue to use and build on Rewarding Environment research and measurement efforts to ensure that a solid, data-based case is made for how and why a Rewarding Environment culture makes a difference to the USGS. Actions should include the following: (a) clarifying the specific organizational outcomes related to Rewarding Environment that are most critical to the USGS, (b) refining the Rewarding Environment model to focus on and measure those outcomes, (c) updating the Rewarding Environment measurement plan, (d) addressing the barriers related to the availability of data, (e) using USGS exit survey data, (f) using the Rewarding Environment priority matrix for identifying organizational priorities, and (g) working with the Employee Survey Program Manager to ensure that appropriate measures and questions are included in the next OAS. The Rewarding Environment Program Manager should continue to use the OAS as a key mechanism for measuring the status of the USGS Rewarding Environment culture change and for engaging employees in conversation about what a rewarding work environment means to them and to the organization. As needed, special topic surveys on Rewarding Environment should be used to supplement the OAS.

6. **Develop a communication plan.** The Rewarding Environment Program Manager should develop a focused, high-profile Rewarding Environment communication plan that uses a variety of opportunities and media to emphasize the definition, goals, and outcomes of having a Rewarding Environment culture as well as those *key components* that have a high impact on a Rewarding Environment culture. The Rewarding Environment Program Manager should promote the current Rewarding Environment Web site by creating a visible link from the internal USGS and People home pages and use creative techniques to communicate and draw attention to USGS success stories and research findings on the impact of a rewarding work environment on science.

7. **Expand Rewarding Environment tools and training.** The Rewarding Environment Program Manager should place additional emphasis on Rewarding Environment tools and training for USGS managers and supervisors. In addition to the brief modules on Rewarding Environment that are presented in the Leadership and Supervisory Challenge courses, a stand-alone course should be developed to explore a rewarding work environment in greater depth. The course should cover the following: (a) the critical components of a rewarding work environment, (b) the link between a rewarding work environment and science, (c) the skills needed to create a rewarding work environment, and (d) tools and strategies that can be used to enhance the work environment. In addition, the coverage of Rewarding Environment that is included in the USGS New Employee Orientation Program should be expanded and the Rewarding Environment concept should be integrated into USGS management, supervisory, and leadership development strategy.

8. **Align Rewarding Environment with other human capital initiatives.** The Rewarding Environment Program Manager should link the Rewarding Environment effort to workforce planning and other key strategic human capital and HR management programs, goals, objectives and initiatives of the Bureau and the Department of the Interior (DOI) to ensure that the Rewarding Environment culture change effort is integrated with other management efforts.

Actions Senior Leaders Can Take To Strengthen the Rewarding Environment Culture at USGS

1. **Review the Rewarding Environment research.** Senior leaders should review the findings from the Rewarding Environment research to gain a better understanding of the role and impact of a rewarding work environment on outcomes of importance to senior management and to the Bureau. Senior leaders should provide feedback and input to further refine the USGS Rewarding Environment model to ensure that the model addresses those outcomes of greatest strategic importance.

2. **Communicate expectations and hold managers accountable.** Senior leaders should communicate the value of creating a rewarding work environment, model the actions and behaviors that contribute to a rewarding work environment, and hold managers and supervisors accountable for creating a rewarding work environment for their employees.

3. **Develop skills of managers and supervisors.** Senior leaders should develop guidelines and standards for use of the USGS management competencies. These competencies should be used for assessing the managerial and supervisory capabilities of individuals before placing them in these positions and for determining their developmental needs once they have been selected. A 360-degree review process also should be implemented to provide managers and supervisors with the full range of feedback regarding their performance and developmental needs.

4. **Recognize managers and supervisors for Rewarding Environment contributions.** Senior leaders should sponsor an award for USGS managers and supervisors who are successful in creating a rewarding work environment and publicly recognize them for their efforts.

5. **Develop guidelines for fairness and equity.** Senior leaders should examine the patterns of Rewarding Environment practices identified in this report and use them as a basis for developing Rewarding Environment guidelines and standards that will promote greater fairness and equity in Rewarding Environment practices across the Bureau.

6. **Support the Rewarding Environment Program Manager.** Senior leaders should continue to support the Rewarding Environment Program Manager's efforts to engage managers and supervisors from across the USGS in helping to enhance the Rewarding Environment culture of the USGS. It is imperative that senior leaders use their influence, authority, and creativity to help remove barriers and challenges that impede the ability of managers and supervisors to create a rewarding environment culture. Doing so is an investment in USGS employees, in the Bureau's mission, and in our future.

Acknowledgments

The authors gratefully acknowledge the reviews and comments provided by the following peer reviewers (all of the U.S. Geological Survey): Nina Burkardt, Steve Hammond, Joan Ratz, and Natalie Sexton. Their thoughtful reviews and helpful comments contributed significantly to the quality of the final report.

References Cited

Corporate Leadership Council, 2002, Building the high-performance workforce; A quantitative analysis of the effectiveness of performance management strategies: Washington, D.C., Corporate Leadership Council, variously paged.

Dunnette, M.D., and Hough, L.M., eds., 1990–94, Handbook of industrial and organizational psychology (2d ed.): Palo Alto, Calif., Consulting Psychologists Press, 4 v.

Judge, T.A., Thoresen, C.J., Bono, J.E., and Patton, G.K., 2001, The job satisfaction-job performance relationship; A qualitative and quantitative review: Psychological Bulletin, v. 127, no. 3, p. 376–407.

Linkage, Inc., 2009, Change leadership; Tools and techniques for leading downstream and upstream change: Burlington, Mass., Linkage Inc.

Manas, T.M., and Graham, M.D., 2002, Creating a total rewards strategy; A toolkit for designing business-based plans: New York, American Management Association, 352 p. plus CD-ROM.

National Research Council, 2001, Future roles and opportunities for the U.S. Geological Survey: Washington, D.C., National Academy Press, 179 p. (Also available online at http://www.nap.edu/catalog.php?record_id=10069.)

Partnership for Public Service and Institute for the Study of Public Policy Implementation of American University, 2003, Best places to work in the Federal Government; Workplace analysis for the Department of the Interior, Geological Survey: Washington, D.C., Partnership for Public Service.

U.S. Geological Survey, 1999, The U.S. Geological Survey strategic plan; 1999–2009: Reston, Va., U.S. Geological Survey, 8 p.

Appendixes A–F

Appendix A. Methodology

Background

The USGS Rewarding Environment Culture Study was a preliminary and exploratory attempt to use the Organizational Assessment Survey (OAS) data to test the relations among organizational culture variables and outcomes of importance to the USGS. The study also was opportunistic in the sense that the administration of the OAS in 2002 provided a good (although not perfect) dataset for testing hypothesized relations among these variables and outcomes. The following overview of the methodology used in this study is intended to describe how the study was performed, explain why certain analyses were or were not conducted, summarize some of the key limitations of this study, and set the stage for the more comprehensive study of Organizational Excellence, which will build upon the work that is presented in this report.

Nature of Organizational Research

There is a well-established history of research on human behavior and performance dating from the early 20th century. Research on leadership and other organizational factors that affect individual and organizational performance began in earnest during the early years of World War II, focusing primarily on improving the selection and training of leaders and understanding the dynamics of team performance. Since then, much has been learned about the impact of organizational environment (including leadership, management practices, culture, and resources) on individual and organizational performance and other outcomes of interest (such as employee recruitment and retention, customer satisfaction, and the organization's reputation).

Many of the research methods and data analyses techniques used for conducting research on people and organizations were originally adapted from research in the natural sciences. Some of the unique issues in measuring human and organizational behaviors, opinions, and attitudes have since led to advances in research methods designed to address some of the inherent unreliability of measuring people and performance. Further, professional standards for evaluating findings in organizational and human behavior research have been established to reflect the added complexity of understanding and predicting human behavior. For example, correlation coefficients greater than 0.3, which reflect approximately 10 percent of shared variance, are generally considered as a baseline for meaningful relations between variables, which means that being able to predict 10 percent of a behavioral characteristic or outcome is seen as an accomplishment. [Note: as a result of multiple regression analyses, predictor variables in this study were able to account for 44 to 64 percent of the variance in the five outcome variables that were examined.]

Development of the USGS Rewarding Environment Model

There is an extensive body of theoretical and applied research literature focusing on organizational culture and its impact on organizational outcomes such as individual and organizational performance, employee satisfaction and engagement, and employee recruitment and retention. Whereas the specific questions, statements, and scales used to test the USGS model were drawn from the 2002 OAS, the basic elements used in the model itself flow directly from this research literature.

For example, the USGS model incorporates the important role that leadership and management practices have been shown to play in defining and reflecting the culture of the organization. In addition, aspects of the organization itself (such as its vision, resources provided to get the work done, and nature of the products and services provided) that have been shown to impact organizational performance and outcomes were also included. Finally, individual variables, such as work satisfaction, tenure, occupational group, age, and other factors, were examined to determine the impact of these individual characteristics and the degree to which findings can be generalized across employee populations.

The USGS model hypothesizes that these factors that contribute to having a Rewarding Environment culture will contribute to *valued outcomes* for the USGS and for employees. Again, such links between organization culture and performance outcomes have been firmly established in the organizational research literature.

Use of the 2002 OAS

The 2002 OAS was only one of the multiple measures of culture and outcomes that were planned for and included in the measurement plan for Rewarding Environment. Because of a variety of data availability issues, however, the OAS became the primary measure used in this study.

The 2002 OAS questions and statements were first grouped into theme and topic areas based on their content. Themes and topics were then categorized into the *key components* of the Rewarding Environment model. Each concept was measured by an index composed of a number of OAS questions and statements representing the following constructs: leadership and management practices, the organization, USGS science vision, the work itself, and *valued outcomes*. Only six of the OAS questions and statements could be categorized as related to *valued outcomes*, with four of the five outcomes being measured by only one OAS question or statement each. The decision to use a single OAS question or statement is justified through previous research that has shown that some measures based on a single question or statement can be quite reliable and valid over time (Dunnette and Hough, 1990–94).

Data Analysis

The sampling framework consisted of all current employees of the USGS at the time the survey was administered. A census was taken of USGS employees; 52 percent (5,355) of USGS employees responded to the survey.

Several rounds of analyses were conducted as part of this study. First, group differences in employee responses to the OAS questions and statements were examined (see table 2). Although group differences were noted on some OAS questions or statements, there was no significant pattern of group responding that ruled out use of the overall Bureau data.

Once the OAS questions and statements were sorted into themes, topics, and categories (see above), OAS question and statement scales were constructed for each of the *key components* of the USGS Rewarding Environment (RE) model. Internal reliability estimates on these scales were then run to ensure that the scale measures were internally consistent. (Cronbach's á for each scale is reported in appendix F.) Only 2 of the 14 scales had reliability coefficients less than 0.75 (0.73 and 0.62, respectively).

Once OAS question and statement scales were constructed, calculations were made to determine the strength of the correlation of each *key component* with employee responses to the OAS statement: "Overall, I find the USGS a rewarding place to work." The correlation is shown beside each *key component* in figure 5. Multiple regression analyses were then used to test the predicted relations between the *key component* scales and the *valued outcome* scales. The percentages of variances accounted for in each of the *valued outcomes* by the combined *key component* scales are shown in the *valued outcome* boxes in figure 5.

Finally, science centers were rank ordered by employee ratings on the OAS statement "Overall, I find the USGS a rewarding place to work," and a "high and low" comparison group profile was developed. The results of that analysis, highlighting the differences between the top- and bottom-scoring science centers, were then tabulated (see table 5).

Research Limitations

Several key research limitations resulted from the primary reliance on OAS data. First, all variables were measured using the same instrument, which introduces common method variance that may exaggerate the strength of relations reported. In addition, it could be argued that employee perceptions are not the most valid or reliable measure of some of the organizational outcomes used in this study. Since no objective or external measures of these outcomes were available, however, the OAS data presented the best available option for at least a tentative look at the relations between Rewarding Environment culture and *valued outcomes* at the USGS. While a low response rate is one of the most frequent sources of bias in social research, the 52-percent response rate in this study was deemed sufficient. In addition, when compared to USGS statistics, there are no major demographic differences between those who responded and those who were less inclined to do so. Finally, having only one OAS question or statement per *valued outcome* for four of the outcome measures means that a heavy reliance is placed on these single-question measures. Overall, and given that this was an exploratory study only, these limitations were seen as acceptable. These issues, however, will be important considerations in the planned follow-on research on Organizational Excellence and science outcomes at the USGS.

Planned Research

Since the research on Rewarding Environment culture and outcomes was conducted, the USGS has developed an Organizational Excellence (OE) model, which is an expanded model of organizational performance focused on Organizational Excellence and its relation to critical science outcomes at the program, Bureau, and societal levels. A second phase of research on Organizational Excellence and science outcomes at USGS is being planned. This second phase of research will utilize an expanded set of measures of the key predictor variables included in the OE model, in addition to results from the next OAS, and will link those measures to science outcome data independent of the OAS. In addition, strategies will be developed in an attempt to increase the response rate in future studies. The planned research on Organizational Excellence and science outcomes will allow the USGS to take an additional step forward in understanding the organizational factors that enhance or inhibit the organization's ability to deliver science.

Appendix B. 2002 Organizational Assessment Survey (OAS) Rewarding Environment Scales

OAS Questions and Statements Used in *Key Component* Predictor Scales

USGS Science Vision

16. I value the leadership provided by the Executive Leadership Team (ELT)/senior leadership.
54. Senior leadership has provided a compelling vision and direction to guide the Bureau into the future.
56. The science vision for USGS takes good advantage of the Bureau's unique mix of science disciplines.
57. Moving toward more integrated science will improve the Bureau's ability to add value to our customers and to society overall.
59. The Bureau is changing in ways that will enhance the Bureau's science impact, science excellence and science leadership.
60. The new program planning process provides adequate opportunities for input from USGS scientists.
61. Scientists in USGS are able to identify and pursue opportunities to work with other scientists across disciplines.
62. The Bureau's science vision is being effectively implemented through its science programs.
63. The USGS is effectively overcoming "turf issues" and other barriers to working with other disciplines.
67. The USGS is making the investments necessary to ensure the long-term viability of its science.
82. I believe that USGS will take corrective action based on the results of this survey.

Leadership and Management Practices

Communications

11. I am kept informed of Bureau-level policies and strategies.
12. Employees are kept informed on issues affecting their jobs.
19c. How effective is management at your science center/office with these leadership behaviors: communicating?
20. Managers/supervisors communicate the organization's mission, vision, and values.
55. The Bureau's science goals and science vision have been communicated to employees at my science center/office.

Performance Management

13. I know who to go to when I need a decision made beyond my own level of authority.
19b. How effective is management at your science center/office with these leadership behaviors: being and holding others accountable?
22. Employees are held accountable for achieving positive results.
23. I receive feedback from my supervisor on how well I am performing.
24. Supervisors clearly communicate what they expect from employees in terms of job performance.

Rewards Practices

3. I feel recognized and rewarded for my contributions to USGS.
4. Employees are recognized and rewarded for working together in teams and across functional or organizational boundaries.
5. Employee contributions are recognized, communicated, and celebrated.
7. Employees are rewarded for providing high-quality products and services to their internal and/or external customers.

Fairness and Respect

1. Recognition and rewards are based on merit.
19a. How effective is management at your science center/office with these leadership behaviors: respecting others?
29. Disputes or conflicts (for example, between co-workers, management and employees) are resolved fairly.

36. In my science center/office, resources (people, funding) are generally allocated fairly and equitably.
43. I believe that Bureau management is committed to treating USGS employees openly and fairly in meeting the Administration's competitive sourcing requirements.

Risk-Taking

15. Employees are encouraged to ask questions and seek out the information they need to do their jobs.
17. The USGS values leadership.
18. Risk-taking is encouraged without fear of punishment for mistakes.
27. Creativity and innovation are encouraged and rewarded.

Managing Diversity

32. The USGS practices zero tolerance for discrimination against employees based on gender, race, color, national origin, religion, age, cultural background, sexual orientation, or disability.
33. In the last several years, the Bureau has made real progress in its efforts to increase the diversity of its workforce.
34. In my science center/office, decisions about people (e.g., rewards, training, assignments, promotions) are made without regard to gender, race, color, national origin, religion, age, cultural background, sexual orientation, or disability.
35. I feel confident that I can bring issues dealing with allegations of prejudice or discrimination to my manager/supervisor/team leaders and these issues will be dealt with.

Quality-of-Worklife Flexibility

74. In my science center/office, supervisors/team leaders try to give employees the flexibility they need to meet family/personal life responsibilities.

Overall Supervision

19g. How effective is management at your science center/office with these leadership behaviors: collaborating?
21. Management in my science center/office is creating an environment that fosters and supports science excellence.
25. My supervisor creates an environment that supports employee involvement, contributions, and teamwork.
26. The Bureau's goals and priorities are being used as a guide when important decisions are being made.
28. My supervisor makes informed decisions and follows through on them.
30. My supervisor has the skills and training needed to do his/her job effectively.
31. Overall, how good of a job do you feel is being done by your immediate supervisor?

The Organization

Resources

38. I have access to the data and information I need to do my job.
39. I have access to the information technology tools and resources I need to do my work on a day-to-day basis (e.g., web access, email, teleconferencing).
40. USGS scientists have the scientific instrumentation and technology capabilities they need to do world-class science.
47. How would you rate your current work place environment on:
    a. Adequate to do the job
    c. Contributing to your productivity

Operational Support

41. "Red tape" and unnecessary rules/regulations do not interfere with the completion of work in a timely manner.
42. The necessary operational processes and practices are in place to help me do my job effectively.

Skills and Training

68. Employees receive the training they need to perform their jobs (for example, on-the-job training, conferences, workshops, coaching/mentoring).

69. My workgroup is keeping up with the changing skills required to do our jobs.
70. My supervisor puts a priority on making training and development opportunities available to employees.

Security and Safety

44. The USGS has taken adequate measures to ensure the security of my work place.
45. There are adequate resources dedicated to ensure information technology security in the USGS.
47. How would you rate your current work place environment on:
    b. Physical health and safety

Products and Services

48. Employees have a good understanding of who their customers are.
49. There are well-defined systems for linking customers' feedback and complaints to employees who can act on their information.
50. Information collected from customers is integrated with other key data and used to improve the quality of products and services.
51. My science center/office effectively delivers data and information to our customers when, where and how they need it.
52. Our customers are well informed about the work that we are doing and the contributions that we are making.

The Work Itself

2. My job makes good use of my job-related skills and abilities.
6. In the work I do, I feel that I am directly contributing to the science mission and accomplishments of the Bureau.
10. I understand how my work contributes directly to the USGS mission.
58. There is a clear link between the work my work group does (science or science support) and the Bureau's science vision.

OAS Questions and Statements Used in *Valued Outcome* Scales

Rewarding Environment

8. Overall, I find the USGS a rewarding place to work.

Morale & Commitment

9. Overall, morale at my Science Center/Office is very high, high, average, low, very low, don't know/not applicable.
14. Employees at my science center/office take pride in being part of the USGS and are strongly committed to the Bureau's mission.

Ability to Recruit and Retain

71. My science center/office is able to compete for and retain the talent it needs in today's marketplace.

Science Vitality

64. Considering its talent base, its science programs, and its science infrastructure, the USGS rates high in health and long-term viability as a scientific organization.

Customer Satisfaction

53. How satisfied do you think your organization's customers are with the products and services they receive?

Appendix C. 2002 Organizational Assessment Survey Responses to Rewarding Environment Write-In Question

What is the ONE most important thing that managers and/or employees at your location could do to make USGS a more rewarding place to work?

Representative Comments by Theme

Rewards Practices

- Be continuous in recognition throughout the year (thank you and good job counts); too often August is the time of monetary awards, which are given to ALL (not just the high performers). So timing is off as well as application.

- Make rewards and recognition a public thing. It is now basically an underground system.

- Rewards and recognition are meaningless many times. In other words--it's OK to provide a poor work environment all year long, but oh--by the way--good job!?

- To make USGS a more rewarding place to work managers can provide employees with written performance appraisals annually and oral assessments of performance at least once during the year. At these points managers can help employees to develop to their full potential by providing further training or varied duties. Also managers can see what is required to help employees to reach optimal performance and thereby help employees feel that they are an asset to the staff. With this type of interaction it should be easier to see when rewards are well deserved. Employees will also be able to see whether they are appreciated for their contributions. My experience has been that going an extra step (even in the right direction) sometimes does more harm than good. The recognition is not there and consequently rewards are absent or only token at best.

- Increased recognition for (1) effective communication of accomplishments and opportunities with customers, (2) leveraging USGS and outside capabilities and resources, and (3) development of research partnerships with other agencies and organizations that support program goals (including international level, where appropriate).

- At our center, non-Primary Investigator scientists (MS-level) are prohibited from moving beyond a GS-09 level, regardless of their productivity (publication rate, amount of funding secured, etc.). Many very good scientists have left this center because they have felt unappreciated by management, and could find better paying work elsewhere.

Opportunities and Support

- They could learn to lead. There is no leadership in the library where I work. Management cannot seem to prioritize work or set policies. We are not a team. I don't get the overall administrative support from my direct line manager or from the USGS administration to do my job properly.

- Perform BASIC managerial duties. (Communication of goals/expectations, feedback on performance, completion of performance reviews, provide guidance or training to perform duties, etc.)

Fairness and Respect

- The most important thing in my particular office would be to act more fairly in the assignment of tasks and projects, because that is where the employee gets the experience needed to apply for promotional opportunities. The managers in my area mold the employees they are friends with by assigning specific projects and then making experience in those projects mandatory for the job opportunities.

- The managers at the top need to be more visible to all employees (such as eating in the cafeteria) and realize that employees down to the cleaning engineers appreciate being recognized with the minimum of a nod or hello when being passed in the hall, in the elevator or anywhere else in the building. Often I've observed that managers look through their employees or away so that they do not have to speak. They should take a lesson from ****.

- Think that a rewarding environment is really about how we treat our colleagues and communicate on a daily basis. It is not just dollars at the end of the year.

- Don't hand out awards to people for doing what is normal, everyday business for the rest of the staff. It's demeaning to those of us who put in extra hours routinely just to get the job done.

- Make sure all people in a group effort are rewarded not just one...technicians count too. If it wasn't for us the work wouldn't get done and done well and as a result those supervisors would not be receiving those awards. So they need to give credit where credit is due. This center is great for awarding the supervisors who didn't do any work, just served as the figurehead and forgetting to award the technicians who actually did the work!! Another thing, supervisors should check the accuracy of the work people are doing before awarding rewards. An instance here at the Center an employee was given a $1500 STAR Award for her WNV research work, but then a month later was outed by fellow technicians for reporting bad results. Makes the supervisor and the Center look bad for rewarding bad work habits, doesn't it?

Communications Issues

- Communicate more clearly objectives/goals and recognize and celebrate our positive efforts and outcomes in reaching those objectives.

- Making communication with employees a priority, helping managers and supervisors develop their communications skills, and holding them accountable for communicating with their employees about the work, their performance, and their accomplishments.

- As a young USGS employee, I find that communication and information dissemination resembles an inverted pyramid with me at the point. The "what" makes it to me, but very often the "who" and most importantly the "why" fail to. Rewards come when knowing how and when one's contributions play a positive role in the science of the USGS.

- Communicate down as well as up and out.

Funding Issues

- In my current job, rewards are given appropriate to employee contributions, successes and accomplishments. However, in most other organizations, there is often too little $ available to give awards to people. The lack of funds only leaves awards that are way too small to be meaningful.

- Improve and increase the rewards to a more reasonable level and improve the timeliness of these rewards. Budgets are not large enough to reward in any meaningful way.

- Focus and fund on Science rather than diverting science funds to new Bureau Regional Staff. This has caused the biggest morale problem in my unit. We see money flowing away from science with no accountability.

- Provide project funding on time and don't constantly change rules on funding. It would help if salaries were taken out of the project budgets and only OE was considered.

- Offer reassurance that our declining budget will not impact our future at USGS. It has been very difficult for 3 to 4 years dealing with a constant threat of furloughs and RIFs because the center's funds are inadequate to support our salaries. We spend more of our time tracking and worrying about the budget than doing the work that is important to support Science. This same situation is occurring in other Federal agencies where budget becomes more of a focus than the work that is important to the role of the organization. Morale is rock bottom. We feel that USGS wants to just get rid of us after threatening us to move to another center or that money is not available to support our salaries. It is very difficult to work in an organization where you are unsure of your future. I have many years invested in the USGS and I hopefully will have many more to come. When I joined the USGS, it had the best reputation in the mapping business.

Reorganization Issues

- Quit reorganizing to offer employees stability.

- Refrain from making sweeping organizational changes, i.e., reallocation of resources, etc., without direct ground level input first.

- Stop reinventing the USGS every couple of years.

Flexiplace Issues

- Allow all employees to work flexiplace...not just a few people.

- Allow flexiplace, but to make it known that it is not for all employees or may not work for all employees. Managers should not take away the option/privilege just because it is not working well for another employee.

- Be consistent on who gets to work at home, including those that work from their home and the office is located outside the geographic area.

- For those employees whose work is possible to be done at home (virtual office) it should be encouraged. My job requires me being in the office very little, yet I am not encouraged on a Bureau level to work from home.

- Track Flexiplace. Report successful use of flexiplace to other employees and investigate other candidates for flexiplace. Advertise statistics on flexiplace, flexitime, maxiflex.

We Already Do a Great Job

- Our managers and employees do a lot of recognition of others through formal (STAR awards) and informal (small gifts, lunch, food) rewards. We have developed a reputation for living the concept of rewarding environment.

- My organizational unit is a rewarding place to work. No improvement is needed to make it more rewarding.

We Need To Focus on the Big Picture

- I personally believe I provide a rewarding environment for my employees. Overall for me the one thing that would make USGS a better place to work is if people could focus more on the big picture and not feel compelled to complain about every little thing. I have worked lots of places and USGS is by far one of the most focused on providing a rewarding environment.

A-76/Privatization Issues

- Eliminate the reality and perception that contracting technicians and scientists is a good resource management personnel policy for the USGS. Contracted positions are more expensive to provide, provide less benefits to the employees, and do not provide the incentives that develop loyalty and commitment (ownership) of project/Bureau goals by these entry level scientists and technical staff.

- Assure us that our jobs are secure, and that our science is important. This is especially true in light of the future danger of privatization of our highly trained govt. scientists.

Appendix D. Rewarding Environment (RE) Measurement Plan

[Terms: AWS, alternative work schedule; FPPS, Federal Personnel-Payroll System; OAS, Organizational Assessment Survey; OPM, Office of Personnel Management; QWL, quality of worklife; SES, Senior Executive Service; TBD, to be determined]

Metric	Measure	Source of data
RE success factors:		
RE is valued by USGS leaders and managers	Actions taken Resources allocated to RE RE aligned with other programs Use of RE measures (future) RE Practices Survey (future)	Training, implementation status reports, success stories Awards, contract, staff time, training time, etc. Leadership, Supervisory Challenges, OAS, Orientation, Mentoring Programs Feedback from managers Survey results
Key elements of RE culture are in place at USGS	OAS Awards distribution/expenditures Use of QWL programs	Specified OAS question/statements Awards distribution/expenditure data Flexiplace, AWS, and other QWL data (from FPPS and OPM survey)
Managers and supervisors are held accountable for creating an RE	Manager/supervisory training data RE included in manager/supervisor performance plans Managers/supervisors rewarded for creating a rewarding work environment (future)	Supervisory Challenge and Leadership course attendees SES and non-SES manager/supervisor performance plans Awards granted to manager/supervisors for creating a rewarding work environment
RE outcomes:		
Employees regard the USGS as a "rewarding place to work"	OAS	OAS questions 3, 8
Employee morale and commitment are high	OAS	OAS questions 9, 14
RE enhances ability of USGS to attract, motivate, and retain a highly qualified workforce	Hiring and attrition in occupational groups OAS Exit survey (future)	Workforce planning data OAS questions 6, 71 Exit survey results
USGS science vitality	OAS Other measures TBD (future)	OAS question 64
Customer satisfaction	OAS (employee perceptions) USGS customer satisfaction data (future)	OAS question 53

Appendix E. "Best Places To Work" Analysis of 2002 Federal Human Capital Survey Comparison of U.S. Geological Survey (USGS), Department of the Interior (DOI), and Federal Governmentwide Responses[1]

Question or statement	USGS	DOI	Govt-wide	80th percentile Govt-wide[2]
Leadership and management practices: Rewards practices				
How satisfied are you with the recognition you receive for doing a good job?	51.9	54.0	54.3	59.4
Employees are rewarded for providing high-quality products and services to customers.	51.0	51.8	51.5	58.2
High-performing employees in my work unit are recognized or rewarded on a timely basis.	48.3	48.9	49.4	56.5
Our organization's awards program provides me with an incentive to do my best.	39.8	42.0	43.8	49.2
Leadership and management practices: Fairness and respect				
Awards in my work unit depend on how well employees perform their jobs.	53.0	52.8	52.2	57.6
Complaints, disputes, or grievances are resolved fairly in my work unit.	52.7	53.8	53.4	56.7
Selections for promotions in my work unit are based on merit.	52.1	50.4	46.2	52.2
Leadership and management practices: Risk-taking				
Creativity and innovation are rewarded.	50.2	50.0	49.3	55.6
Leadership and management practices: Overall supervision				
Overall, how good a job do you feel is being done by your immediate supervisor?	65.2	65.9	65.9	69.9
Supervisors/team leaders in my work unit encourage my development at work.	61.5	62.4	61.3	65.5
Supervisors/team leaders in my work unit provide employees with the opportunities to demonstrate their leadership skills.	58.1	59.9	59.3	63.0
Supervisors/team leaders are receptive to change.	53.0	53.3	54.8	57.8
Leadership and management practices: Performance management				
Managers review and evaluate the organization's progress toward meeting its goals and objectives.	64.1	64.6	66.7	69.6
My performance appraisal is a fair reflection of my performance.	61.8	64.3	64.0	69.3
Discussions with my supervisor/team leader about my performance are worthwhile.	59.3	62.8	61.0	64.5
Information collected on my work unit's performance is used to improve my work unit's performance.	55.8	57.4	59.3	62.2
Leadership and management practices: Communication				
I have enough information to do my job well.	68.7	66.9	67.9	70.5
Managers promote communication among different work units.	53.7	53.9	56.0	59.3
How satisfied are you with the information you receive from management on what's going on in your organization?	51.4	52.5	53.0	56.5

[1]Partnership for Public Service and Institute for the Study of Public Policy Implementation of American University, "Best Places to Work in the Federal Government: Workplace Analysis for the Department of the Interior, Geological Survey," November 2003.

[2]Of 189 organizations surveyed in the 2002 Federal Human Capital Survey, 80 percent fell below the "80th percentile" score for any given question. These "80th percentile" scores are presented as benchmarks for agencies that are striving to improve their scores.

Appendix E. "Best Places To Work" Analysis of 2002 Federal Human Capital Survey Comparison of U.S. Geological Survey (USGS), Department of the Interior (DOI), and Federal Governmentwide Responses[1]—Continued

Question or statement	USGS	DOI	Govt-wide	80th percentile Govt-wide[2]
Leadership and management practices: Managing diversity				
Managers/supervisors/team leaders work well with employees of different backgrounds.	66.1	65.6	65.5	68.4
Policies and programs promote diversity in the workplace.	65.3	66.3	65.6	68.9
Supervisors/team leaders in my work unit are committed to a workforce representative of all segments of society.	62.6	64.3	63.8	67.0
The organization: Skills and training				
The workforce has the job-relevant knowledge and skills necessary to accomplish organizational goals.	67.2	67.5	67.2	70.9
I receive the training I need to perform my job.	62.9	62.4	61.5	66.4
The skill level in my work unit has improved in the past year.	61.5	62.7	61.5	64.0
I am given a real opportunity to improve my skills in my organization.	61.5	62.2	61.2	65.5
My talents are used well in the workplace.	61.2	62.4	61.6	64.0
My training needs are assessed.	55.3	53.0	56.0	59.5
Science vision and leadership				
My organization's leaders maintain high standards of honesty and integrity.	54.1	57.0	56.1	61.7
I hold my organization's leaders in high regard.	47.5	51.4	52.9	57.3
The work itself				
The work I do is important.	81.0	83.0	83.2	84.4
I know how my work relates to the agency's mission and goals.	79.2	80.1	79.8	82.0
I like the kind of work I do.	78.7	79.1	77.3	78.9
My work gives me a feeling of personal accomplishment.	69.4	69.8	68.6	70.8
My job makes good use of my skills and abilities.	65.7	64.7	63.8	66.1
Rewarding place to work				
Considering everything, how satisfied are you with your job?	68.9	68.0	67.3	69.5
I recommend my organization as a good place to work.	66.1	65.9	62.5	67.3
How would you rate your organization to work for compared to other organizations?	67.4	65.1	62.5	67.3
Considering everything, how would you rate your overall satisfaction in your organization at the present time?	58.7	59.4	59.3	63.1
Motivation and commitment				
In my organization, leaders generate high levels of motivation and commitment in the workforce.	43.6	46.5	47.2	50.5
Ability to recruit and retain				
My work unit is able to recruit people with the right skills.	47.7	50.6	48.6	55.6

☐ **Higher** than 60 percent favorable responses

▨ **Lower** than 45 percent favorable responses

Appendix F. 2002 Organizational Assessment Survey (OAS) Measurement Model for Rewarding Environment: Summary Table

[Terms: α, Cronbach's α, a measure of internal consistency of items in the scale (1.0 = perfect internal consistency); CS, customer satisfaction (as perceived by employees); M&C, morale and commitment; NA, not applicable; r, scale intercorrelations, a measure of relation between scales and outcomes (1.0 = perfect correlation); RE, Rewarding Environment overall; R&R, ability to recruit and retain; SV, science vitality]

OAS *key component predictor scales*			Correlations with *valued outcomes* (r)				
	OAS question or statement number	α	RE	M&C	R&R	SV	CS
USGS science vision	16, 54, 56, 57, 59, 60, 61, 62, 63, 67, 82	0.91	0.44	0.48	0.42	0.63	0.31
Leadership and management practices							
Communications	11, 12, 19c, 20, 55	0.83	0.50	0.58	0.42	0.39	0.38
Performance management	13, 19b, 22, 23, 24	0.80	0.52	0.58	0.41	0.33	0.40
Rewards practices	3, 4, 5, 7	0.88	0.67	0.58	0.43	0.34	0.34
Fairness and respect	1, 19a, 29, 36, 43	0.81	0.63	0.65	0.47	0.36	0.38
Risk-taking	15, 17, 18, 27	0.81	0.62	0.65	0.45	0.44	0.40
Managing diversity	32, 33, 34, 35	0.83	0.45	0.45	0.33	0.28	0.35
Quality-of-worklife flexibility	74	NA	--	--	--	--	--
Overall supervision	19g, 21, 25, 26, 28, 30, 31	0.91	0.56	0.61	0.42	0.33	0.41
The organization							
Resources	38, 39, 40, 47a, 47c	0.79	0.46	0.47	0.43	0.40	0.38
Operational support	41, 42	0.77	0.38	0.37	0.33	0.39	0.22
Skills and training	68, 69, 70	0.84	0.47	0.46	0.48	0.30	0.38
Security and safety	44, 45, 47b	0.62	0.30	0.32	0.29	0.27	0.26
Products and services	48, 49, 50, 51, 52	0.87	0.34	0.42	0.38	0.38	0.63
The work itself	2, 6, 10, 58	0.73	0.57	0.54	0.32	0.35	0.38

Appendix F. 2002 Organizational Assessment Survey (OAS) Measurement Model for Rewarding Environment: Summary Table—Continued

[Terms: ά, Cronbach's ά, a measure of internal consistency of items in the scale (1.0 = perfect internal consistency); CS, customer satisfaction (as perceived by employees); M&C, morale and commitment; NA, not applicable; r, scale intercorrelations, a measure of relation between scales and outcomes (1.0 = perfect correlation); RE, Rewarding Environment overall; R&R, ability to recruit and retain; SV, science vitality]

USGS valued outcomes		Correlations with valued outcomes (r)				
	OAS question or statement number	RE	M&C	R&R	SV	CS
Rewarding Environment overall (RE)	8	1.0	0.64	0.37	0.39	0.35
Morale & commitment (M&C)	9, 14		1.0	0.45	0.42	0.38
Ability to recruit & retain (R&R)	71			1.0	0.38	0.31
Science vitality (SV)	64				1.0	0.32
Customer satisfaction (CS) as perceived by employees	53					1.0

☐ ALL correlations reported are statistically significant

▨ High correlations (greater than or equal to 0.45) are highlighted in green